What people are saying about ...

spiritual parenting

"*Spiritual Parenting* paints a marvelous portrait of the environment God wants us to have in our Christian homes. Dr. Anthony has masterfully woven Biblical truth and personal experience together in a way that will instruct and inspire any parent who reads. I believe this is the most comprehensive description of a God-centered home in print today. It's not about techniques (though there are some great ones in the book), but about a mind-set. Read this book, and you will change who you are as a family, not merely what you do. Trust me—when you finish, you will know what being a spiritual parent looks like!"

Larry Fowler, executive director
of Global Training, Awana

"With refreshing honesty, Michelle Anthony shares her wisdom about parenting from a perspective *everyone* can relate to. While keeping a real-world perspective, she weaves a picture of how we can guide our children not just to be 'good' kids, but to be active and vital members of the family of God. Her own life lessons give you a sense of vision for what your parenting can become. Her honest and transparent illustrations will inspire you to excel in your role as a mom or a dad."

Ken Canfield, PhD, executive director, Boone
Center for the Family, Pepperdine University

"There is no doubt in my mind that this book will help you be a more effective parent and bring you an abundance of practical help. Michelle Anthony is one of America's premier leaders in the field of family and parenting. *Spiritual Parenting* is one of the best books I have ever read on energizing your family's spiritual life as well as presenting a philosophy of parenting worth living out. It will make a legacy of difference in your parenting."

Jim Burns, PhD, president of HomeWord
and author of *Creating an Intimate
Marriage* and *Confident Parenting*

"My thoughts as I read *Spiritual Parenting:* 'Wow! I never thought of it like that! That actually sounds *doable.*' Michelle Anthony has written a biblical, honest, encouraging, complete work that is different from any other Christian parenting book I've read. Generations can be changed by the power of God through the principles in this book."

Rob Biagi, recording artist

"How I wish I had this amazing, insightful book long before my first day of parenting! Michelle's unique perspectives and practical wisdom have encouraged, challenged, and inspired me in the immensely important task and privilege of raising my children to truly know and love the living God. I believe millions of families and churches will be powerfully affected by this book! It is an absolute must-read for Christian parents!"

Jana Alayra, Christian praise and
worship recording artist for children

spiritual
parenting

spiritual parenting

an awakening for today's families

michelle anthony

transforming lives together

SPIRITUAL PARENTING
Published by David C. Cook
4050 Lee Vance View
Colorado Springs, CO 80918 U.S.A.

David C. Cook Distribution Canada
55 Woodslee Avenue, Paris, Ontario, Canada N3L 3E5

David C. Cook U.K., Kingsway Communications
Eastbourne, East Sussex BN23 6NT, England

David C. Cook and the graphic circle C logo
are registered trademarks of Cook Communications Ministries.

All Scripture quotations, unless otherwise noted, are taken from the *Holy Bible, New International Version*. *NIV*. © 1973, 1978, 1984 by International Bible Society. Used by permission of Zondervan. All rights reserved. Scripture quotations marked MSG are taken from *THE MESSAGE*. Copyright © by Eugene H. Peterson 1993, 1994, 1995, 1996, 2000, 2001, 2002. Used by permission of NavPress Publishing Group. Scripture quotations marked NASB are taken from the *New American Standard Bible*, © Copyright 1960, 1995 by The Lockman Foundation. Used by permission. The author has added italics to Scripture quotations for emphasis.

LCCN 2010921503
ISBN 978-1-4347-6447-8
eISBN 978-1-4347-0221-0

© 2010 Michelle Anthony

The Team: Don Pape, Karen Lee-Thorp, Caitlyn York, Karen Athen
Cover design: Amy Kiechlin
Cover images: iStockphoto, royalty-free

Printed in the United States of America
First Edition 2010

1 2 3 4 5 6 7 8 9 10

032910

To my children: Chantel and Brendon.

You are the reason I want to
be a spiritual parent!

Thank you for letting me tell "your
stories" and for sharing your lives;

It is a privilege to be your mom.

I thank God for you everyday!

Contents

1

In the Path of the Divine

Beyond Managing Behavior

Too much of our time is spent trying to
chart God on a grid, and too little is
spent allowing our hearts to feel awe. By
reducing Christian spirituality to formula,
we deprive our hearts of wonder.

Donald Miller[1]

In the Path of the Divine

As a young parent, I wanted to do a good job raising my children. Well, if I'm honest, I wanted to do a perfect job! I hated to fail, and I definitely didn't want to fail at this. I wanted people to look at my kids in amazement and think, "Wow, what a magnificent mother!" I became overwhelmed with trying to please everyone with my parenting. It was exhausting.

Both my mother and my mother-in-law were stay-at-home moms in the 1950s and '60s. They were like Mary Poppins: practically perfect in every way! Who can compete with that legacy? I wanted them to think I was cutting it with their grandchildren. But it didn't stop there. I'd be at a church event, and I'd want the ladies at my table to think I had it together so they wouldn't see how scared I felt. I was even beginning to care what the grocery clerk—a perfect stranger!—thought of me as a parent.

Of course, part of that was my pride, but another part was that I didn't want to do the parenting thing wrong, or badly—or even worse, to not do enough. I loved my children, and I wanted the best for them.

I have a close friend who one day joked, half-seriously, that she was setting aside a little money every month while her kids were little, so that someday they could pay for counseling (because of the dysfunction she was surely imposing on them)! Now, while we may laugh at her thought process, we also may understand how my friend felt. In that statement she was identifying how important her role as a parent truly was, for better or for worse, to her children's well-being for their entire lives.

In this book we will explore what it means to seek God as our primary audience—to please Him alone with our parenting and seek Him alone for the strength and power to do so. Spiritual parenting is not perfect parenting—it's parenting from a spiritual perspective with eternity in mind. It's a way of parenting that declares, "I want to parent the child or children that God gave me in such a way that I first honor God, and then second, create the best environment to put my children in the path of the Divine."

What does it mean to put my child in the path of the Divine? Only God is divine. His divinity is the essence of His holiness, which ultimately transforms each of us. Through Jesus and His work on the cross, God transfers His holiness to me. Wow! What an incredible thought! This transaction takes place by God's grace and through my faith, of course, but how it actually happens is a mystery.

As spiritual parents, we enlist ourselves as students of our children … to learn about them specifically as the children God has entrusted to us. Not only do I need to learn how to rely on God (since His Word makes it clear that He alone is the one who changes hearts), but I also need to learn how my children are fearfully and wonderfully made in order to best guide them on the path that God has designed specifically for each one. It's not about adopting a "parenting style" that works for all my children, because I will need to adapt my parenting to the *uniqueness* of each child (while still retaining my authority and values).

Parenting Crisis 101

I remember having a crisis of parenthood one day when my daughter was only four. God was about to teach me a powerful lesson. He wanted me to learn some unique facets of my daughter's temperament while revealing to me how much I needed His help in order to shape her heart toward Him.

She was in her room playing with something. I told her to clean it up so that we could have lunch. She came out of her room, defiant, and started talking back to me. Soon we had entered into an epic battle of the wills. I was telling her to do something, and she wasn't doing it. She was also very verbal in her resistance. It was one of those moments when I felt I needed to win—but I didn't know how.

So I told her, "You need to go to your room right now to have a time-out, because you are not obeying me."

She took an unyielding stance. Her body language said, *I'm not going, and what are* you *going to do about it?*

I repeated myself firmly: "You need to go to your room right now. You need to obey your mommy."

And then she looked at me and said, "No. I don't have to do what you say because you're only *third* in charge." She went on to explain that first God was in charge, then Daddy, and *then* me. I knew then that we were going to have our hands full with this one! She was strong, opinionated, passionate, and articulate. So I did what any rational woman would do in my situation—I called "second in charge."

On the phone with my husband (even though he was at work), I sobbed about how horrible *his* four-year-old daughter was being to me. I was tattling. He listened patiently and then gently said, "Honey, she's four. You're the adult."

She finally went to her room—screaming and crying. *I* was screaming and crying. I felt like a total failure as a mom. A four-year-old had gotten me to lose my cool and behave at her level. I decided it was time to talk to "first in charge." I prayed. I told God I felt defeated as a parent. I didn't feel equipped for this. And I didn't know how I'd do it differently if this happened again—and I knew it would.

Parenting "Aha!"

Since God's Word makes it clear that He alone is divine and He alone changes hearts, I knew I needed Him to help me parent differently. I knew I would have to parent with His goal in mind if I was going to be successful. Pleasing Him became my only focus that day. Nothing else mattered.

This was the first truth I began to cling to in my desire to be a spiritual parent. This truth revealed to me that *it was not my job to merely control my child's behavior and by doing so somehow create a spiritual life for him or her.* This was a real "Aha" for me. Nowhere in the Bible does God ask me to spend my days managing the deeds and actions of my child. Nowhere in Scripture am I warned that if I don't "control" my child's behavior, horrible things will happen.

However, I have oftentimes assumed this role—and sometimes pursued it as an end in itself. After all, who doesn't want children who behave beautifully at all times? For years I had naively assumed that as Christian parents we simply have babies, raise them in a Christian home, and then do our best as parents. We expose them to Christ and to God's Word, we put them in the community of other believers, and then eventually … don't they just choose to follow Him?

Igniting a Transforming Faith

That day was a defining moment in my role as a spiritual parent, because I didn't feel prepared to deal with my daughter's strong will, and I certainly didn't feel equipped to pass on my faith to either of my children. It was one thing for me to make sure that I taught them Bible stories and took them to church on Sunday mornings. I felt confident that I could teach them good morals and values and could for the most part keep them away from the dangers of this world. I even knew I could intentionally expose them to godly people and benevolent causes. But if my job was not to merely control my children's behavior in these matters, then what was it?

I realized that my goal was much more grand than I had imagined—much more compelling. My goal was to pass on a vibrant and transforming faith, the kind of faith in which:

- My children would *know* and *hear* God's voice, discerning it from all others.
- They would *desire* to obey Him when they heard His voice.
- They would *obey* Him not in their own power, but in the power of the Holy Spirit.

One question still lingered. It haunted me in my depths. How would I pattern my parenting in such a way that these things I knew were essential would ignite in my children vibrant, spiritually transforming faith?

I longed for a place where I could talk about these things and be enlightened and equipped. This book is birthed out of that longing. Here you'll read some of my own experiences and how God's Word and Spirit shaped my thinking and actions while I raised my children. We'll ask questions such as, "At the end of the day, how can we feel confident that we invested in what *really matters most?* In fact, what does 'matter most' mean in our constantly changing, pressurized world?"

Whether we are single parents or part of a blended or traditional parenting model, the most significant part of our lives—and our children's lives—is our spiritual health. In fact, researcher George

Barna once stated that every dimension of a person's life experience hinges on his or her moral and spiritual condition.[2] Think about it: What you believe and where you aim your heart determines the direction and outcome of your entire life for eternity. Read it again: *What you believe and where you aim your heart determines the direction and outcome of your entire life for eternity.* Eternity is at stake.

Jesus said our purpose as God's people is to love Him with our whole life and to love others in every way we can think of (Luke 10:27). Furthermore, our purpose as parents is to teach our children about the awe-inspiring wonder of who God is, how to have a relationship with Him, and what it looks like to live our lives for Him and through Him. These are the purposes we'll aim for in this book.

In the World but Not of It

As a young mom I was putting all of my efforts into shielding my children from this world, keeping them from wanting or desiring the things of the world, whether it be a movie I didn't want them to watch or a bad word I didn't want them to say. As they got older, I focused on making sure they weren't taking drugs or having sex before marriage. I was spending far too much energy on keeping them from the things I deemed harmful or sinful (essentially doing my best to control their behavior) because I was scared.

Oftentimes parents, recognizing the evil in the world, determine to take their child out of it completely. They say, "I'm going to pull them in close. I'm going to protect them from immorality. If I do this, the world won't negatively affect them." So they hold their children really, really close and really, really tight in an attempt to shield them from what is threatening.

Some other parents say, "You know what, my kids are eventually going to need to be toughened up by the world." And these parents simply push their children into it, almost like throwing a child into the deep end of the pool and saying, "They'll learn how to swim eventually." These parents often rationalize this approach by their own journey. One father told me, "I'm not sure what the big deal is with raising kids. I was practically raised by wolves, and I turned out okay—and here I am back in church. I have a good life now. It all evens out eventually, right?"

Neither of these extremes is biblical. The Christian life calls us to be *in* the world but not *of* it. Yes, in the one extreme our children are not, in all probability, "of" the world. Certainly, they don't bear the stench of the world as much as their counterparts—but as we attempt to separate them from it, they are not "in" it either. And the other extreme? Well, they're probably so much "in" it that they do bear the marks of sin. The stench of the world can overwhelm their spiritual vitality.

Spiritual parenting doesn't ignore the world's depravity. But spiritual parenting also does not say, "Hunker down and hide— merely endure it to the end. Because the world is so evil, I don't want any part of it." Rather, I propose that spiritual parenting proclaims, "I'm going to stand here in the midst of it all. I'm going to live *in* the world because God has placed me here in it for this time. I do this, and yet I recognize that we are *aliens*, as the apostle Peter states. This world is not my home. It never will be. I will never feel completely comfortable here. I will never feel that I truly fit in. So while I'm here, I'm not going to be *of* it." This is where spiritual parenting becomes important. It determines, through

God's help, how we will live productive and spiritual lives here and yet not become comfortable in the world around us. Really, this dependence on God and His Spirit is at the heart of being a spiritual parent.

When I was first wrestling with this concept, I was afraid. I felt there was absolutely no way I could do that. I didn't feel I could expose my children to this world without the sin and stain of this world damaging them in horrific ways. It was such a natural reaction to want to protect them from that.

How We Define Ourselves

Maybe some of you are like me. Raised in a Christian home, I often felt defined by the things that I *didn't* do. To *not* smoke, *not* drink, *not* swear, *not* chew, and *not* go with boys who do (such a helpful little rhyme) was how I defined myself for the most part. But what would it look like if we parented a generation of young people to define themselves by what they *did* do? What if they were defined by their actions of justice and mercy, forgiveness and love, strength and courage, generosity and humility and faithfulness? What if they were a generation who lived in the world and still proclaimed these things by their very lives?

The danger in merely focusing on our children's outward behavior without the inner transformation is that sometimes our children will align their behavior to our mandates to please us or receive approval. They can end up doing or not doing these things without true spiritual healing inside. Without this supernatural transformation, we may have moral or obedient children, but we don't necessarily have spiritual children.

Before long, after the external motivations for obedient behavior are eliminated, our children will grow up and determine life for themselves. Either they will have been transformed by God's Spirit, they will have chosen to live sinfully without any desire to change, or they will hide their sin and live a double life. But a spiritual life is one that is transformed and out of hiding.

Strangely Dim

Now what if we as spiritual parents agreed to do something different than merely manage our children's behavior? *What if we put our energy toward setting our children in the path of the Divine and watching them fall in love with Jesus?* What a remarkable difference this would make! One option warns, "Don't fall in love with the world," while the other option offers, "Fall in love with Jesus, and the world will look less attractive."

When I was little I used to sing a song in church, and I have come to understand these words in richer and more meaningful ways during my adult life:

> *Turn your eyes upon Jesus,*
> *Look full in His wonderful face,*
> *And the things of earth will grow strangely dim*
> *In the light of His glory and grace.*[3]

I have realized how profound these words are in my life and in the lives of my children. The song doesn't direct me to turn away from the world, but rather to turn to Jesus. Just as the author of Hebrews calls us to "fix our eyes on Jesus, the author and perfecter of our faith" (Heb. 12:2), the charge is to look to *Jesus*. When I do this, the world suddenly grows dim in its allure, and I begin to love it less as I love Jesus more.

Living Testaments

What better way to have our children fall in love with Jesus than for us to be living testimonies of what that means? One thing is true in spiritual parenting: *You can't give away something you don't have!*

Let me illustrate this: I have been rock climbing before, and I really enjoyed it. I did a good job at following directions, but I am certainly a novice on the ropes. Now, if I were to offer to take you rock climbing on one of the highest gorges in the world and be your instructor, I can pretty much guarantee that you wouldn't be willing to do that. You would wisely recognize that I can't teach you to do something that I don't understand the fundamentals of myself. Yet often the mind-set we embrace as parents is based on our desire for our children to have a more vibrant spiritual relationship with Christ than we ourselves are currently experiencing.

Think about it. We want so much for our children. We want them to have a better education than we did. We want them to have better opportunities. We want them to have life a little easier, with less struggle or pain. In general, we want them to have *more* than we had. We are guilty even of sometimes wanting them to have a more genuine spiritual life than we do. But the fact is that we are living examples of what is real, and unfortunately, we can't give away something we don't possess.

So spiritual parenting reminds me that it's not my job to merely control my children's behavior, but rather it is my job to model with authenticity *what I have* in my relationship with God through Christ. And hopefully what I have is worth passing on to the next generation.

Natural Flow of Life

Our children hunger to see the reality of who God is in the natural flow of our lives—when we're getting up, when we're sitting down, when we're on a journey, when we're putting them to bed. It's not that the formalized methodology is bad, because it definitely has a place. It's just that it's not *best* apart from a role model. Our children need to see that faith matters, that it's relevant to our daily situations, that it's real. We need to model how our lives are spiritual in every decision, erasing the divide between sacred and secular. They need to witness firsthand that our faith is not merely something we compartmentalize when it's convenient to do so.

Some of my best moments of sharing the reality of God with my children were ones I didn't plan. They just happened. There were days when money was tight and we prayed for God to provide. Then we waited. And without our expecting it, a refund check from the insurance company arrived in the mail. There were times when we were held up from traveling somewhere because a neighbor needed our assistance, only to find that we were spared from an accident on the highway that occurred just moments before.

Other days were filled with trips to the zoo, where my son was so amazed by the diversity of the animals that he asked me, "Who thought of that?" Questions about why there is a rainbow in the sky after it rains, what the story of the Bible is, where God lives, where people go when they die, why we give money at church, why we pray or sing or worship—all of these become natural teachable moments of sharing our faith with our children when we generously live it in front of them.

Behavior as a By-product

In order to pass on our faith to our children, we need to understand what biblical faith is and how it is connected to action. We'll deal with this at length in chapter 2, but for now let me point to what James writes in the Bible about faith. He alerts us that our faith without works is dead (James 2:14–26)—as lifeless as a body without the spirit inside it. It's simply dead. So faith in our lives and in our children's lives must have this expression of obedience for it to be alive. Perhaps the fullest definition of faith comes from its meaning in the original Greek. The word *pistos* embodies three things: possessing a *firm conviction,* making a *personal surrender,* and demonstrating the *corresponding conduct.*

Now remember that one of the nonnegotiables for spiritual parenting is that it's not my responsibility to control my child's behavior. However, this definition of faith supports that when one possesses a firm conviction and a personal surrender, then the corresponding behavior, inspired by the prior two, will follow. Wow! *This* is where behavior comes in.

Too often we merely focus on the "corresponding behavior" part, missing the point that it is a by-product. This by-product is the outcome of a *firm conviction* (which is something we probably most intuitively know about faith), but it's also from a posture of *personal surrender.* This aspect of surrender is something we don't always acknowledge in our own lives, let alone teach to our children. In simple terms, faith is based on a strong belief from a heart of self surrender.

Thus, behavior isn't something we simply manage—otherwise our Christianity is nothing more that what Dallas Willard refers to as "sin management."[4] How compelling is that? Rather, when we see our behavior and that of our children as a by-product of genuine faith, we begin to understand what it means to pursue a spiritual life and spiritual parenting.

Cultivating Environments

Faith is supernatural. I am not capable of creating it in another person. I can give you all the information about something, and you can still not believe or experience an unwavering conviction. We can probably all think of someone who has been exposed to the truth of Scripture and of God and yet still doesn't believe. It takes a supernatural transformation. Just as belief and trust that produce faith in a person's life are a supernatural transaction, the behavior and action that align with faith need to flow supernaturally. When we try to manufacture this or impose it on others, they become resistant or even rebellious.

Believe it or not, this is where freedom comes in. As we put our children in proximity to God, to fall in love with Jesus, the Holy Spirit is the one who makes their actions congruent with their belief. He's the one who causes the process of their hearts to become more and more like Jesus'. This is true transformation. As their faith is vibrant, their actions become vibrant. So often our temptation as parents is to spend all of our time and energy striving to fix their behavior—a process that is not our responsibility.

What is our job then? The joy of parenting can be spent on cultivating environments for our children's faith to grow, teaching them how to cultivate a love relationship with Jesus as we cultivate our own, living our lives authentically in front of them so that they become eyewitnesses to our own transformation.

As a young teenager, I heard my dad get up early every morning to go downstairs. I never heard the TV or heard busyness in the kitchen, but one day I saw what he had been doing down there every morning. He was kneeling, praying, and reading God's Word. I can't remember my dad ever telling me I "should" read my Bible, but it was modeled for me quietly and consistently—and that was captivating to me. Understanding our part in this process of spiritual parenting is foundational for us before we embark on the rest of this book.

Discovering My Role as a Parent

At its core, then, *Spiritual Parenting* is not merely a book on "how to parent." It's far more than that. It's a book about how to view your *role* as a spiritually minded parent, the God-given role that is yours alone. Essentially, it asks the question, "What is my end goal in raising each of the children God has entrusted to me, and then how will I parent them with that end in mind?"

With this perspective, I can take my focus off of a series of day-to-day events and set it on the bigger picture of passing on my faith. Each moment of every day becomes an opportunity to parent toward my God-given goal. I parent in a way that does not simply *spend* my hours but also allows me to *invest* my days toward eternity.

This book is designed to inspire you—to awaken you, if you will, toward a greater perspective about the spiritual role of parenting. As you see that role revealed and as the Holy Spirit works through that insight, then God will give you the guidance to apply these truths to specific situations that come up in your home. I hope the question, "Who does God require me to be as a parent, and how will I create environments in my home for Him to be at work in the unique children that He has entrusted to me?" will resonate over and over in your heart as you read these pages.

Our goal as parents should be to endeavor to pass down our faith to the next generation in such a way that they will be able to pass down their faith to the following generation in our absence. Someday we won't be here, and all that will remain is that which is eternal—those things that we have successfully transferred to our children, and our children's children, so that faith will endure to all generations.

2

What's the Rock?

A Transforming Faith

We can conclude that faith, as an
affair of the heart and a commitment
of the mind that results in service
and spiritual behavior, is a very close,
personal relationship with God.

Merton Strommen and Richard Hardel[5]

What Is God Looking For?

If we want our faith to endure for all generations, we must become increasingly confident and focused about the kind of faith we are trying to pass on to our children. Think about it for a moment: How would you define your own faith? What is it exactly? I've heard people say that their faith is an enduring belief that is resilient, growing, and developing, while others say that it is simply knowing that

God is going to do exactly what He said and that He's going to do it regardless of the situation and circumstance.

I think that we would all agree with these descriptions. We can even recognize that faith is a choice, and although it can seem foolish, especially to others who are watching, we simply know it's about something real. But to me, there is more. Deep down, I know that there is this part of faith that requires me to act or respond if I'm really going to be transformed.

Let's look at what God has to say about faith. First, when Jesus speaks of His imminent return in Luke 18:8, He says, "When the Son of Man comes, will he find faith on the earth?" This is a really compelling verse for me because the God of this universe, the Holy God, is telling me the *one thing* that He'll be looking for upon His return.[6] I mean, it's almost too simple. He actually told us what it was. He said, "I'm going to be looking for faith. Will I find it?" He could have said a myriad of things, but He said *faith*.

I don't know about you, but when I was young and my mom left for the day, she would often say, "Michelle, your room is a mess. By the time I get home today, I really want that room to be cleaned up, okay?" And then she'd leave. Later, I'd get home from school, and I might be watching TV until I heard that car come up the driveway. Then I would think, "Uh-oh … my room!" I would race up the stairs and throw things in my closets and under my bed because I knew that it would be the first thing my mom would ask me about when she came in the door. She had given me specific instructions on what she expected. She said, "I want you to clean your room," and she expected upon her return that I would have completed the task she had given me to do. She expected that I would *respond* to her words of authority.

In a similar way, Jesus asks, "Will I find faith on the earth?" Then I respond by acting on this while I am here on earth. This endeavor becomes preeminent above anything else I could possibly be pursuing, because I know He will expect it from me when He returns.

Faith through the Family

Second, in Psalm 78 we find a blueprint of God's grand method for faith replication throughout all generations. He chose to use the *family* as the primary place to nurture faith. The psalmist Asaph unveils God's plan:

> I will open my mouth in parables,
>   I will utter hidden things, things from of old—
> what we have heard and known,
>   what our fathers have told us.
> We will not hide them from their children;
>   we will tell the next generation
>   the praiseworthy deeds of the LORD,
>   his power, and the wonders he has done.
> He decreed statutes for Jacob
>   and established the law in Israel,
>   which he commanded our forefathers
>   to teach their children,
> so the next generation would know them,
>   even the children yet to be born,
>   and they in turn would tell their children.
> Then they would put their trust in God
>   and would not forget his deeds

but would keep his commands.
They would not be like their forefathers—
    a stubborn and rebellious generation,
whose hearts were not loyal to God,
    whose spirits were not faithful to him. (vv. 2–8)

This is a beautiful psalm that shares God's intent for the family and for each generation to pass on their faith to the next. So, not only did He say that faith was the primary thing that He would expect from us someday, but He also set up an infrastructure that He envisioned would be best for this type of replication: the family.

I grew up in a Christian family. I grew up hearing that my great-grandfather was a preacher around the turn of the previous century and that my father's grandfather told my father stories of his own faith in Jesus—and that nothing else mattered in life. I watched my grand-parents spend half of each year in the U.S. fund-raising so that they could spend the other half of the year in India providing education and spreading the gospel to the poorest of the poor. My uncles, aunts, and cousins also lived lives that taught me something of what it means to be a follower of Jesus. And of course my parents, who received this heritage, were then entrusted to pass it down to my sister and me.

I often wondered how that must have felt for them to inherit such a huge responsibility! I watched my mother live out the words she taught. Her life was an example of integrity and beauty. My father lived in humility and generosity. Then I became a parent. Now it felt even *more* ominous.

I didn't want to be the one who broke the chain—the weak link who was unable to pass the baton to the next generation in the great relay race of life! Of course, my parents weren't perfect. They made their fair share of mistakes. But they were real. They chose to live out their faith even when it was messy, and they chose to walk that path openly and honestly with me. So I chose to follow in their footsteps when I became a parent. My kids can tell you that I am far from perfect, and they can recite the times when I have failed them and God. But God's design doesn't require perfection—it requires faithfulness.

Perhaps you didn't have such a heritage. Perhaps nothing was handed to you in the form of a spiritual baton, and you are beginning this race as the first generation of faith. How exciting! Just think that someday, one of your great-great-grandchildren will sit down to recount how *you*, their ancestor, were a God-fearing and faithful example, and without your faith they wouldn't have been the same. Imagine the impact that your faith will have on history!

Faith in Action

In addition to the master plan outlined in Psalm 78, we have accounts in the Gospels where Jesus experienced faith in others, and when He did, He was *amazed.* He stopped and applauded it every time He witnessed it. At times when He observed faith in action, it appears that He was even surprised. In fact the only time recorded in Scripture when Jesus was amazed was when He encountered a Roman centurion's faith on display. "I have not found anyone in Israel with such great faith," He said (Matt. 8:10). He always acknowledged it, always responded to it, and always blessed it. Likewise, when Jesus expected to see it and didn't, He would chastise, "O you of little faith!" Faith is a really big deal to our God. And He's given us the commission to pass it on to our children.

In chapter 1 we learned that the biblical definition of faith states that a firm conviction and personal surrender will manifest itself in corresponding behavior. James writes,

> What good is it, my brothers, if a man claims to have faith but has no deeds? Can such faith save him? Suppose a brother or sister is without clothes and daily food. If one of you says to him, "Go, I wish you well; keep warm and well fed," but does nothing about his physical needs, what good is it? In the same way, faith by itself, if it is not accompanied by action, is dead.

> But someone will say, "You have faith; I have deeds."

> Show me your faith without deeds, and I will show you my faith by what I do. You believe that there is one God. Good! Even the demons believe that—and shudder.

> You foolish man, do you want evidence that faith without deeds is useless? … As the body without the spirit is dead, so faith without deeds is dead. (James 2:14–20, 26)

James is cautioning us against adopting a solely intellectual belief system of biblical knowledge and the things that we *say* we believe. At the same time, however, there are other places in Scripture where we see Jesus condemning people (the Pharisees among others) for simply *doing things* in the flesh but not actually being led by the Spirit or by His power to do those things. It's not about just "doing good stuff." Jesus made this point when He gave the example of how we are to cling to and abide in the Vine.

I Can Do Nothing

Jesus said, "I am the vine, you are the branches; he who abides in Me and I in him, he bears much fruit, for apart from Me you can do nothing" (John 15:5 NASB). We are the branches. He is the Vine. The vine is the plant's food source. It is the way the branches are nourished with nutrients and water, which bring life to the budding fruit. Apart from Him we can do nothing. He instructs us that as we abide, then and only then will we bear fruit. There's also a caution in this for us to not just do "good stuff" without the power source that makes it good: God. I love the visual embedded in this passage.

Recently I was in Temecula, California, which is known as beautiful wine country. There are vast and picturesque vineyards as far as the eye can see. The imagery of the vineyard and what it means to bear fruit has always been intriguing to me. As I drove down the road that day, I saw something that stood out to me, a visual expression that I will never forget.

On one side of the road was a beautiful vine that almost looked fake because it was so perfect. It was a picturesque vine abounding with huge clusters of luscious grapes. Grapes still on the vine are a magnificent sight! Underneath these vines, somebody had painted on a wooden board the words, "Abide in me and you will bear much fruit." In contrast, on the other side of the road stood a lonely, withered branch. It was lifeless, its leaves dead, and it just looked pathetic. Here it stood, just one ugly branch, useful for nothing. A wooden board also accompanied this branch, stating, "Apart from me you can do nothing."

What a great visual! Even the separation of the road told part of the story. The dead branch was completely detached from the vine, with no fruit. What's interesting about Jesus' words is that He says, "Apart from Me you can do *nothing*." The syntax of this sentence doesn't say that you can't do anything (because if you think about it, we can "do" a lot). Jesus is making a *qualitative* statement. He's saying, "Really, in My eyes it amounts to nothing. You can 'do,' but it's nothing." He's making a judgment statement on the value of our works.

So we live in this tension that faith is not just an intellectual assent by itself, but it's not works apart from faith either. It's a blend of intellectual assent and the works that flow from it. Therefore, spiritual parenting involves creating environments for that blend to happen in your home. *How* it happens is a mystery. That's the supernatural work of the Holy Spirit. But we do have a part in it. And if our part is not to control our children's behavior but rather to create a place for the Holy Spirit to do His work, then He's the one who knows how to blend this faith in our minds (the belief system) with the natural outpouring and manifestations (the fruit).

I know these things to be true. In my heart and in my mind, I understand that only God can change lives. But I confess to you that I am tempted daily to simply "try harder" to walk this life of faith. Not only do I find this temptation in my own life, but I also struggle enormously not to impose this false faith on my children by encouraging them to "try harder" as well. How foolish I am when I either try in my own efforts to be transformed, or more foolish yet, when I ignore altogether the path that He has set out for me!

The Two Foundations

Do you remember the parable of the two foundations that Jesus told? The one where the wise man built his house on the rock and the foolish man built his house on the sand? If you were raised in church, you may have not only heard it but learned a song about it as well. This parable is recorded in Matthew 7:24–27. A wise man built his house on a rock, and when the rain and storms came, his house stood firm. Then the foolish man built his house on the foundation of sand, and when the rain and storms came upon this house, it was utterly destroyed. Jesus was making a distinction between the two foundations.

If this story tells of such dramatic implications, it raises the question, "What is the rock?" It's vital to the story that we know what the rock is, since Jesus is giving us a metaphor to instruct us to build our house upon it. Take a moment and think about it: What do you understand the rock foundation to be according to this story? I literally went most of my Christian life thinking that the rock was *Jesus*. I've asked a lot of people, and this is the most popular answer. There are places in Scripture where Jesus is referred to as the Rock, but in this parable He is not. Read the passage below and see if you can determine what the rock is.

> "Therefore everyone who hears these words of mine
> and puts them into practice is like a wise man who
> built his house on the rock. The rain came down,

the streams rose, and the winds blew and beat
against that house; yet it did not fall, because it had
its foundation on the rock. But everyone who hears
these words of mine and does not put them into
practice is like a foolish man who built his house
on sand. The rain came down, the streams rose, and
the winds blew and beat against that house, and it
fell with a great crash." (Matt. 7:24–27)

Obedient Faith

Did you see it? Jesus says that everyone who *hears these words* and *puts them into practice* is like a wise man who built his house on the rock. How would we characterize someone who hears something and then puts it into practice? Obeying. So in this story, the rock becomes obedience. The foundations refer to how someone hears the truth and then either chooses to put that into practice—obey—or chooses not to put that into practice and disobey.

This is the faith and action partnership. It's putting into practice what we believe. It's not simply hearing God's Word—because the foolish man heard it and didn't put it into practice. When we think about parenting from a perspective of passing on our faith to the next generation, then building on rock means obeying God's Word in our everyday circumstances and letting our children be eyewitnesses to that rock-solid way of living.

Proverbs addresses this issue in abundance. In the first few chapters of Proverbs, Solomon instructs his son to live wisely by being obedient to the instruction of God and His way. He charges him to resist the temptation of foolishness, which ignores God and chooses what the world offers instead. Of course as parents, we want what Solomon wanted for his son. We want them to choose God and wisdom. We want them to be grounded on a solid foundation so that when the storms of life beat down hard on them, they will endure.

Faith That Flows from Relationship

Although the kind of faith that Jesus is looking for is obedient faith, from all that we discussed thus far we know that this kind of obedience comes from knowing God and hearing His voice. When we do this, we have a relationship with Him from which a *desire* to obey flows. This obedience is then *empowered* through God's Spirit, not through our own fortitude of trying harder. We take little steps each day to enter deeper and deeper into a relationship with God and to align our will and actions to His. This is obedient faith.

When I was younger I knew it was important to obey. As a child I had many people to obey: my parents, my grandparents, my teachers, our pastors, police officers, and so on. None of these authority figures required me to *desire* to obey them as part of our relationship. The focus was merely on my obedience as an end. "Because I said so" was a common phrase these authority figures used. I got the picture. Just obey and everyone is happy, right?

Well, not so with God. He wanted my heart, too! Jesus even told the crowds who were following Him, "Unless your righteousness surpasses that of the Pharisees and the teachers of the law, you will certainly not enter the kingdom of heaven" (Matt. 5:20). The Pharisees were not lacking in obedience by any measure. No one in

Jewish society followed the letter of the law more than they did. I suspect that Jesus was referring to the righteousness of His followers not being something *quantitatively* more than that of the Pharisees, but rather being something *qualitatively* more. He wanted obedience of a different kind.

Certainly when our children are little we want them to simply trust and obey us. Things such as don't touch the stove, run in the street, or talk to strangers are boundaries to protect their very lives. Yet as our children mature, we need to help them move from sheer behaviorist obedience to obedience out of wisdom and relationship—trusting that we know best. This is the kind of faith we're talking about. As parents we will need to not only introduce this concept but model it. It's unlike any obedience they will encounter during their earthly lives, yet it has eternal ramifications.

Creating Space for God's Spirit to Be at Work

If we believe that the Holy Spirit is God's chosen teacher in our children's hearts and that He is the one who causes spiritual growth when and as He chooses, then we must be willing to cultivate environments for Him to do this work. So how can we as parents create environments in our homes that will allow our children to not only hear God's words but also have an opportunity to put them into practice? In this book we'll look at ten distinct environments that we can create in our homes. As we seek to create these spiritual spaces, we will pray that God's Spirit will transform our children into His likeness.

I've dedicated a chapter to each environment in order to explain what it is and then to describe the ways it can be expressed in your home and in your children's lives. Here is a brief explanation of these ten environments:

1. **Storytelling.** The power of the *Big God Story* impacts our lives by giving us an awe-inspiring perspective into how God has been moving throughout history. It compels us to see how God is using every person's life and is creating a unique story that deserves to be told for God's glory.

2. **Identity.** This environment highlights who we are in Christ. According to Ephesians 1, we have been chosen, adopted, redeemed, sealed, and given an inheritance in Christ. This conviction allows children to stand firm against the counter-identities that could seduce them away from God in this world.

3. **Faith Community.** God designed us to live in community and to experience Him in ways that can happen only in proximity to one another. The faith community creates an environment to equip and disciple parents, to celebrate God's faithfulness, and to bring a richness of worship through tradition and rituals that offer children an identity.

4. **Service.** This posture of the heart asks the question, "What needs to be done?" It allows the Holy Spirit to cultivate sensitivity to others with a cause that is bigger than an individual life. It helps fulfill the mandate that as Christ-followers we are to view our lives as living sacrifices we generously give away.

5. **Out of the Comfort Zone.** As children are challenged to step out of their comfort zone from an early age, they learn and experience a dependence on the Holy Spirit to equip and strengthen them beyond their natural abilities and desires. This environment inspires a generation to seek not comfort but a radical life of faith in Christ.

6. **Responsibility.** This environment enables children to take ownership of their lives, gifts, and resources before God. In addition, children are challenged to take responsibility for their brothers and sisters in Christ as well as for those who are spiritually lost. Our hope is that the Holy Spirit will use this environment to nurture each child within a kingdom-minded worldview, from a place not of burden but rather of one who has been entrusted with a great calling.

7. **Course Correction.** This environment flows out of Hebrews 12:11–13 and is the direct opposite of punishment. Instead, biblical discipline for a child encompasses (a) a season of pain, (b) an opportunity to build up in love, and (c) a vision of a corrected path with the purpose of healing at its core.

8. **Love and Respect.** Without love, our faith becomes futile. This environment recognizes that children need an environment of love and respect in order to be free to both receive and give God's grace. Innate in this environment is the value that children are respected because they embody the very image of God. We must speak *to* them not *at* them, and we must commit to an environment

where love and acceptance are never withheld because of one's behavior.

9. **Knowing.** Nothing is more important than knowing and being known by God. We live in a world that denies absolute truth, and yet God's Word offers just that. As we, through personally knowing God, create an environment that upholds and displays God's truth, we give children the assurance of being known by God through a relationship with Him in Christ.

10. **Modeling.** Biblical content needs to be expressed in practical living in order for it to make a difference spiritually. Knowing is the "who," while modeling is the "how." This environment is a hands-on example of what it means for children to put their faith into action.

Now that we understand what faith is and what our goals as parents are—and aren't—we have a foundation for talking about these environments. It's crucial that we don't create environments for our children to simply look religious on the outside. We don't create environments to manipulate their behaviors. We don't even create environments so that they'll have an amazing belief in Christ. We're creating environments so that we open our homes and our children's lives to the Holy Spirit, so He can do His work in them.

In Philippians 2:13, Paul reminds us that it is *God* who is at work within each of us, working out His will. So even putting into practice the things we have heard comes from God Himself. Our job and our privilege is to place our children in the path where He is at work. We get to come alongside where He is already moving. We get to place them in proximity to the Divine and then let the Divine do the supernatural in their lives. It's such an honor. It really is.

So as we start looking at these ten environments, let me ask you to do a couple of things:

1. Take some time to pray and ask God to reveal to you the things He wants to shape in you as a mom or a dad and in your home. Let Him tenderly bring to your awareness the areas where you need a shift in thinking, responding, or listening. You will need this posture for the entirety of this book. You were never asked to parent alone. As a Christian parent, you have been given the resource of partnering with the Spirit of God to raise your child. We must always remember that it is God who is at work in our children's lives, and we simply have the privilege of coming alongside Him in that endeavor (Phil. 2:13).

2. I believe that as you assume this posture, God will speak to you and work in your life and in your home. What's really fun about having this kind of learning environment is that we're all learners, including me, and we invite the Holy Spirit to come and be the teacher. So anytime you feel like God gives you an "Aha," or you put some dots together in a way that's really big for you, you can write it in the "Aha" pages that are provided for you at the end of this book (see page 217). I hope you will pause and look into each "Aha" as God brings it to your attention. At the completion of this book, these may be the most significant discoveries in your journey as a parent.

3

A Garden and a Big White Horse
The Environment of Storytelling

At the heart of our Christian faith is
a story.... Unless the story is known,
understood, owned, and lived, we and
our children will not have Christian faith.

John H. Westerhoff[7]

A Child's Little World

When I was a child, I used to love when my father told me stories at bedtime. Not just any story either. I always wanted him to tell me a story that had *me* as the main character. Usually my father wove in a few of my other friends (and perhaps foes), and maybe even a childhood pet as well. With these thoughts of myself as the heroine or adventurer in my father's stories, I drifted off to sleep knowing that all was right in my little world.

As children, our world is very small. We see *everything* from our vantage point and how it affects us directly or indirectly. It's only as we mature (hopefully) that we begin to see the world as much more complex, and we begin to see our role as servants addressing the needs of those around us. Therefore, one role of the Christian parent is to train our children to shift from self-centeredness to other-centeredness. Paul describes this virtue in Philippians 2:3–4 (NASB): "Do nothing from selfishness or empty conceit, but with humility of mind regard one another as more important than yourselves; do not merely look out for your own personal interests, but also for the interests of others."

Of course, this selflessness comes from knowing Jesus personally and committing our very lives to the power that is available to us from God. Yet even before our children fully understand this war within, I believe that the environment of storytelling is a compelling opportunity to begin to shape an other-centered and God-centered worldview in their hearts.

I know that to some degree childhood is synonymous with ego-centrism. With self-absorption raging in the hearts and minds of our children, how can we help them understand that there's a story line much bigger than they are? How can we parent in such a way that tells the Big God Story throughout history, explains how our own story has been grafted in by grace, and describes how our children have the opportunity to be a part of that narrative as well?

A Bigger Story

While today's culture is telling our children that life is "all about me," we can direct them to think about the fact that life is really "all about God." God's Word is basically a love story—a story of the lover pursuing His created ones in order to have a personal relationship with each one of them. In His story, *He* is the main character; *He* is the perfect Lover and the perfect Redeemer.

Sometimes I am tempted to believe that *I* am the main character, that the story is really about me—because after all, I am in every scene. But that's a lie. It's a lie that our children are told on every TV channel, in every advertisement, and in every song. Sometimes it's blatant and sometimes sublime, but nonetheless they are being made to believe that the greatest story ever told is happening in their obscure little world.

Can you see how dangerous Satan's lie is? If he can get me to believe that this life is a story centered around me and my happiness, then I will see life as a series of events that allow me either to succeed or fail in this endeavor. I begin to subtly make decisions that will be to my own benefit. After all, don't we always want the main character to be victorious in the end? We want her to succeed and be happy. Thus, my happiness becomes primary. The problem with this perspective is that life is hard and unfair sometimes. I can't always control life, events, and other people. Then what? And even when I do manage to control people, that's not what I or they were created for. In using them to make my life work, I harm them.

If we consistently tell our children the Big God Story and help them to see the bigger story that has been lived out for thousands of years, they will have the privilege of catching a glimpse of the wonder of it all. The wonderful mystery of who God is and how He has chosen a part for each of us to play. We can never play the role of the main character, but when we understand why we can't, we rest in the knowledge that we were never created to do so. When this happens, we are able to worship God and not ourselves. We are free to be who we were created to be: true worshippers in every aspect of our lives!

I love how the apostle Paul says this in Romans 12:1–2 (MSG):

> So here's what I want you to do, God helping you:
> Take your everyday, ordinary life—your sleep-
> ing, eating, going-to-work, and walking-around
> life—and place it before God as an offering.
> Embracing what God does for you is the best thing
> you can do for him. Don't become so well-adjusted
> to your culture that you fit into it without even
> thinking. Instead, fix your attention on God. You'll
> be changed from the inside out. Readily recognize
> what he wants from you, and quickly respond to it.
> Unlike the culture around you, always dragging you
> down to its level of immaturity, God brings the best
> out of you, develops well-formed maturity in you.

Okay, great concept, but how does that really play out in our daily lives of raising our kids? Let's take a few moments to unpack this and to see how we can effectively begin to set our children up for success in this area. We will first take a look at the Big God Story and how to share it concisely with God as the redeeming thread throughout. Next, we will investigate how our own story has inter-sected with that story and see the power of telling those truths to our children. And finally, we will consider practical activities that will help us reinforce the truth of Scripture in our children's lives.

Children are a precious gift from God and bear the indelible stamp of God's image. This brings such incredible significance to our mission of raising them to know Him.

The Big God Story

In chapter 2 we discussed the God-given roles of parenting and the commission that God gave us to raise our children to know and love Him. In light of this, how can we tell His story—the story of the Bible—in a way that is meaningful and relevant to our children? We know our children are self-absorbed, and yet we also know they love the sense of story and are eager to identify with heroes in a story line. God's Word gives us no shortage of material that illuminates the struggle between good and evil, and certainly no shortage of heroes! We also know that they relate best to things that are concrete and visual, and to circumstances that involve their five senses.

With this in mind, let's consider sharing the Bible's content in the context of its original story line. Often we tell fragmented stories of God, Jesus, or other characters in the Bible, and we do so in ways that aren't linear. Even most children who know the stories of the Bible can't tell you whether Abraham was born before David, or if baby Jesus was alive when baby Moses was.

Think of the little girl, who had celebrated Christmas just three months earlier, sitting in an Easter service where the pastor talked about Jesus dying for our sins. Horrified, the little girl looked at her daddy and exclaimed, "Didn't God have any big people to die? Jesus is only a little baby!"

What happens is that our stories are told in isolation and often don't tell the bigger story where God is central. Instead, baby Moses is the key figure one day, Noah is the key figure one day, and Jesus is merely the key figure on another occasion. But by putting each story in context of the main story, we can begin to elevate Jesus, the Redeemer, to His rightful place in the story line.

Let's examine this main story line and understand what it would look like if we told it in its essence.

The Lineage of the Redeemer

The Big God Story began in a beautiful garden nestled between four grand rivers. God created this garden and named it Eden. He created Adam and Eve to be in relationship with Him and to live in this beautiful garden together along with all of God's creation. Unfortunately, Adam and Eve sinned against God. Therefore, God told them to leave the garden and the intimate relationship they once shared with Him. This is called the fall of Adam and Eve. But in the midst of this tragedy, God promised that one day a Redeemer would come. This promised Redeemer would save humanity from sin and disobedience. And so, mankind began to wait in expectation for the promise to be fulfilled.

Within just ten generations, the world had become so evil and corrupt that God decided to destroy all people, except for Noah and his family, through a global flood. After the water subsided, Noah's family began to repopulate the earth, and nations were birthed from each of Noah's three sons. The nation of Israel would eventually arise from Noah's son Shem.

God gave a unique promise to a descendant of Shem named Abraham. This promise was that, through Abraham's son, God would set apart a nation that would demonstrate the relationship between

God and humanity. As other nations saw this love relationship, they, too, would want to know the one true God. God also told Abraham that the promised Redeemer would be born out of his family line. This chosen nation would eventually be called Israel.

Abraham and his wife, Sarah, could not have children, so they began to doubt God's promise. They eventually grew weary of waiting for God's timing and unfortunately felt the need to "help God out" by having a son through their maidservant, Hagar. This son was named Ishmael. His descendants became the Arab nations. However, twenty-five years after God promised Abraham and Sarah a son, the promised son was born. They named him Isaac.

Isaac had a son named Jacob. After Jacob wrestled with the angel of the Lord in a dream, God changed Jacob's name to "Israel" (which means "one who strives with God"). Jacob/Israel had twelve sons, and the descendants of these twelve sons eventually became the twelve tribes of Israel.

One of Jacob's sons, Joseph, was sold into slavery by his brothers and was taken to Egypt. There, God allowed Joseph to rise to power under the pharaoh. Eventually Jacob's entire family moved to Egypt. Joseph was able to keep them alive during seven years of famine in the region and by doing so preserved the family of the promise.

From Slavery to Freedom—Over and Over

After several centuries in Egypt, the descendants of Jacob/Israel became a large ethnic group called the Israelites. The Egyptians enslaved them, and they cried out to God for a redeemer. God chose an Israelite named Moses to lead His people out of Egypt and into the Promised Land so they could worship God alone.

However, because of their disobedience and grumblings, that generation of Israelites spent the next forty years wandering in the desert between Egypt and the Promised Land. A generation grew up in the wilderness with a new respect for God and His power. This generation had grown up not being seduced by the powers of thousands of Egyptian gods, but rather seeing the work of the one and only true God daily in the provision of food, water, and guidance. In fact, the only food they had ever eaten was manna, supplied each day by God Himself. God led this generation in the form of a pillar of clouds by day and a pillar of fire by night, so this new generation grew to know and trust Him alone. Joshua was the anointed leader of this young generation, and he led them to conquer the Promised Land that God had set aside for His people.

Through years of battle, the Israelites claimed their land and settled down to raise families. (Today this is the nation of Israel, which occupies the land east of the Mediterranean Sea and northeast of Egypt.) The Israelites cried out to God to give them a king like other nations, and God answered, "No." They disobeyed and wandered away from Him, so God raised up other nations to bring punishment for their sin. When they repented, He sent leaders called judges to help them prevail against their enemies, and for a time they remained faithful to God. But soon they returned to their wicked ways until calamity struck again. This cycle of sin, suffering, repentance, and deliverance happened over and over, and Israel had many judges. This time of the judges, who included Gideon, Deborah, Samson, and Samuel, lasted for over 450 years.

Kings, Good and Bad

Despite God's warning that kings would take the people's money through taxes, their daughters as wives and slaves, and their sons to wars, the people insisted on electing a king. Israel was now a monarchy, and God was no longer her only King.

Saul was first to reign as king, but God quickly rejected him because of his pride and disobedience. David, a humble shepherd boy who knew and loved God, followed as the second king. He sometimes sinned badly, but he remained "a man after God's heart" because he was humble and loved to worship. His son Solomon became the third and final king of the united twelve tribes.

Solomon's son faced rebellion in the land, and the nation split in two: ten tribes in the north (Israel) and two tribes in the south (Judah). The line of the promised Redeemer now followed the tribe of Judah in the south.

Israel (the ten tribes in the north) had only evil kings who led their people into great sin. Israel was eventually taken captive by Assyria, even after many prophets pleaded with the people to repent. Although Judah (the two tribes in the south) had a few good kings and even several revivals, they, too, disobeyed God over and over until He finally let the Babylonian Empire conquer them. The city of Jerusalem, the center of God's people, was utterly destroyed. The Babylonians took the people of Judah away into captivity.

The Jews in Captivity

Some of the Jews (people of Judah) kept their faith in God alive, even in Babylon. We know of Daniel and his righteous acts of prayer in the midst of hungry lions. We know how Shadrach, Meshach, and Abednego stood strong in the face of pressure to compromise.

Eventually, Babylon fell to the Persian Empire. A Jewish orphan named Esther became queen of Persia, and God worked through her to save her people from death. Also under Persian rule, Nehemiah (a Jewish cupbearer for the Persian king Artaxerxes) returned to Israel to rebuild Jerusalem's walls. The Persian king not only let this happen, but he paid for it too! In all, one of the greatest construction projects of the ancient world was completed in a mere fifty-two days, even in the midst of a great opposition in the land. The lineage of the promised Christ was now back in the motherland of Israel, and the Old Testament came to a close.

Then something strange happened: God was silent. He didn't speak through a prophet, a priest, or a king. The promise was alive, but it was hidden and still. The people waited for the promise to be revealed. Nearly four hundred years passed before the opening words in the New Testament.

The Redeemer Arrives at Last

The lineage recorded for us by Matthew and Luke shows that the same promise that began in the garden remained true throughout thousands of years. Despite Satan's efforts to eliminate the people of God, they prevailed. And at the appointed time in history that had been prophesied hundreds of years before, the Redeemer arrived in an obscure town called Bethlehem.

Jesus was born. He was the Messiah promised in Genesis, predicted throughout history, and finally here on earth in the flesh.

He was born of a virgin, Mary, who raised Him with her eventual husband, Joseph, in the town of Nazareth. Jesus grew in wisdom and stature and in favor with God and men.

When Jesus was grown, His cousin John the Baptist became a voice in the wilderness preparing the way for Jesus the Messiah's ministry. Soon after, Jesus called Peter, James, John, and the remainder of the twelve disciples. He ministered to the poor, healed the sick, raised the dead, and redeemed the outcast. Jesus lived and proclaimed the kingdom of God, demonstrated His divine power over creation, and taught His disciples and the world a radical new way to live.

He became a man for the purpose of being the perfect sacrifice that would pay the price for our sin. The Jewish people practiced animal sacrifice as the price for sin. They made offerings of pure, undefiled lambs for the sins they committed against God, just as God had commanded them in the law of Moses. Jesus became the once-and-for-all sacrifice who gives every man, woman, and child access to God for all time. He was the final sacrifice, satisfying God's justice for all time for all those who accept Him.

His death provided the way for our sins to be forgiven. His resurrection cleared the way for victory over death. His ascension into heaven enabled Him to send the Holy Spirit to abide in us. And His Spirit empowers the church to live out the message of salvation. The book of Acts tells how the Spirit did this in the earliest church in Jerusalem and in the apostle Paul's missionary journeys. Today the Holy Spirit continues to work in each of our lives for the glory of God, allowing each one of us to be a part of His Big Story until He returns.

He's Coming Back!

The story doesn't end with us! It is much bigger than that! Jesus will return. He will return not shrouded by His humanness but completely unveiled in all of His glory. He will ride in victory on His white horse to proclaim that He is King of Kings and Lord of Lords forever. He will judge the nations and eventually send Satan and his followers to an eternity of separation from God. Those who love God and who have accepted His Son Jesus will live with Him in the new heaven and new earth forever, in relationship with God—the way it all began in the garden. The way it *should* be. And from that day on, for all of eternity, we will be with the promised Lord and Redeemer forever and ever. Amen!

A Story Kids Can Relate To

This is the Big God Story. Good and evil war with each other, evil seems to overtake the world, but then Jesus shows up and brings justice ... and we who know Him are saved. He makes everything good, and those who follow Jesus all win in the end! I don't know about you, but I want to be part of *that* story, and I definitely want to be on the winning side. I want to be one of Jesus' friends when He shows up on the scene. And I want Satan to be punished! This is a story that kids can relate to, and yet so often we only allow them to see pieces of it at any given time. We prevent them from seeing the power of it when we do that.

I've often thought that someone needs to make a movie of the Big God Story that kids can watch in two hours. It wouldn't be much different from all the other movies they watch that have the same basic plot of good warring against evil, except for one big difference—this one is *true!* And more than that, each one of us is truly a part of it. It's my story too, and I get to play a part. I choose whose team I'm on, and then I cheer on my team all the way through the story. It doesn't begin when I'm born and end when I die. The story keeps on going until God says it's time to end it. When it ends, we will all be there to witness it! We will all come together and spend eternity worshipping Him and telling how our life played a part in the Big God Story. It is a story about God. It's all about Him. I play a part.

Jesus Is the Hero

In the Big God Story, Jesus is the hero. We all love the Jesus portrayed in the Gospels—in those accounts, Jesus loves us and shows us how to live and love back. He helps us understand who the Father is and how our relationship with Him should be. But in the Gospels, for a kid, Jesus is not the hero. Now don't get me wrong—as adults, we see that He is the hero because He sacrificed Himself for our sin, and He conquered death. But for kids, we need to make sure that we portray both pictures of who Jesus is. He is both Shepherd and King. He is both gentle and warrior. He is both humble and victor!

But oddly enough, we often don't tell our kids about the end of the story—or the beginning. Maybe we think it's too bloody or too intense, or maybe we don't understand it all, but in reality it makes Jesus the kind of hero worth living and dying for. Knowing that He is the ultimate victor gives each one of us the courage to walk with Him on this journey.

Telling Our Story

Speaking of journeys, we all have one. This is what makes *my* story and *your* story unique. You may be asking yourself, so what? Okay, we have these kids who are really into themselves, and we get them to see themselves as part of this bigger story where Jesus is the hero, and just like that something spectacular happens? Well, yes, it does. The simplicity of it is that this can happen.

We can allow our kids to feel the awe of being part of something way bigger than themselves. We can tell them the narrative of history in the context of the big picture, and we can create opportunities for them to put what they are learning into action. Ultimately this can create in them a hunger for more and validate what we are teaching them.

Take a moment and think about *your* story. Think about your beginnings and your family of origin. How did God use the circumstances in your life—both the positive and the negative—to bring you to Himself? At what point or points in your life did you recognize God's intervention? When did you realize that there was more to life than living for yourself? How did that affect the way you lived, spent your money, or interacted with others? How did the Divine intersect with your mortal existence? This is your story. This is the essence of who and why you are. This is a story worthy of telling!

Sometimes in Christianity we call this a testimony. Unfortunately, we have the habit of seeing the miraculous in the testimony of others' lives, not our own. We admire those who have been rescued from the pit of destruction and the claws of deception and abuse. We tend to view the story of one raised in the faith of Christ from an early age as not really a testimony at all.

Someone once commented on my story, which has no single radical moment of life change, by asking me if God was more powerful when He rescued someone from a life of total destruction or when He orchestrated events to prevent that path from ever happening. There is no acceptable answer to this question, because all of God's redeeming work is awesome, whether or not it is classified so by onlookers. We are all sinners, and we all need a Savior. As Christians, we have all been redeemed, and we all have a story.

Storytelling Our Lives

There is power in telling our story to our children. At the earliest age, our children can begin to hear parts of our story and to be eyewitnesses to how God is continuing to shape it. I love to tell my children aspects of my own faith story in the context of the age they are at that time.

For instance, when my daughter was struggling with friendships in the fourth grade, I shared with her how God had worked in my life during the fourth grade in my friendships and what I felt He did because of my dependence on Him during that time of loneliness.

Or, when my son was in middle school, he recognized that he could get by in school without needing to give much effort to his schoolwork. So I recounted for him how I felt about school during my early adolescent years. I told him how God showed me that giving my best in all situations was a character quality that would affect the rest of my life and my faith in general.

Even parents who did not experience a faith relationship with God as children or teenagers can share how the events of their lives at that time led them to come to faith, or how they could have benefited from knowing a God who loved them and had a place for them in the big story He's writing.

The impact of your story on the lives of your children is priceless, because it gives them insight into what's to come in their concrete context of the here and now. Of course God has a different journey for all of us, but as we live and share our faith story, it gives our children the hope of something more, something bigger than the perceived enormity of their present situation.

Our Kids in God's Story

In addition to storytelling the Big God Story and generously sharing our own stories, it's important for us to help our children catch a glimpse of the story line that they are uniquely a part of.

A few years ago, we took our two children to the Dominican Republic on a family mission trip. This is a powerful way for teenagers to see life as bigger than their little world. A mission trip requires them to give of themselves sacrificially, so it combats their intense desire to remain egocentric. They meet people from other cultures and languages who call Jesus their Lord, and they sense their smallness (yet importance) in relationship to the real hero. A mission trip also gives teenagers some concrete experiences they need to make the story line of God's power come alive, so that it becomes a literal part of day-to-day life.

We spent three months preparing for this trip by attending missions orientation and training meetings. In these meetings we each chose serving teams. My son chose puppets, technical support, and drama. My daughter chose drama, crafts, and recreation. Both of them, like everyone else on the team, needed to practice giving their testimony. We gave each person the opportunity to tell their story, and then we celebrated with them. Of course, my children were nervous the first time they gave their testimony, but each time it got easier and easier.

One day while serving in a leprosarium, sharing the gospel with people scarred from the disease of leprosy, I was in awe as I stood back and watched my children. My son was walking up to hug the men and women without hands or arms. He shook the offered stub of a man without hesitation. He played the role of Jesus in the pantomime drama, so gently offering his outstretched arms to those without them.

My daughter sang like an angel that day, songs that she had learned in their language, and she later gave her testimony in front of more than sixty people through an interpreter. I cried. I thanked God. I knew that even if it were only one day, they had captured a part of the Big God Story. That for this moment in time, life was not about them or what they had or did not have, but about Jesus and His love. I will never forget that day, and maybe more importantly, neither will they.

Tell the Story

Simply by telling the Big God Story we can help our kids understand the grand meta-narrative. We can even draw it out on a piece of paper so they can see the sequence of events. They can see what has happened so far and, not unlike reading the last chapter of a book, what is still to come.

When reading or telling a Bible story, we should ask children to place it into the larger continuum and give account for when and where that story took place. We should always give context to what was happening and always make Jesus the Redeemer or God our Father the main character, even when it appears that someone else is.

Finally, as parents, we need to consistently make the Jesus of Revelation known. Make Jesus the hero of your life and your child's life. Jesus loved and loves us heroically, putting His needs and wants aside in order to die for us. He answers prayers heroically, listens heroically, and conquers evil heroically. Each day, eagerly allow your child to anticipate what might happen next in the heroic story line.

I have often told my children before they leave for school, "I wonder how God will show His care for you today, or speak to you about a certain problem through His Word or someone who loves you, or how He will show you His power in creation. Be on the lookout. I don't know how He's going to do it, but He will. Watch for it! Today *you* will be a part of the greatest story ever told."

4

Royal Blood

The Environment of Identity

In J. R. R. Tolkien's *The Hobbit,* the
magician Gandalf told the reluctant
and unlikely hero Bilbo Baggins,
"There is more to you than you know."
He said this, knowing that within the
hobbit's veins coursed blood not only
from the sedentary Baggins side of the
family but also from the swashbuckling
Took side. We have a similar mingling
of blood within us from a lineage that
is both human and divine.... Most of
the time, though, we are burrowed
away in our hobbit holes and don't
give a thought to our heritage.

Ken Gire[8]

Who Am I?

When we start to realize how amazing God's story is, a question naturally arises: "*Who am I* that I should get to be a part of the greatest story ever told?" Think about that question. How would you answer it? Is there a set of right answers that comes to your mind? Or do you struggle with knowing what that really means? Do you have a sense that God, the Creator of all things, created you and me—for a unique purpose? These are the questions that shape the environment of identity. The fact that you and I are even invited to be a part of God's grand narrative of life, love, and redemption is true only because of Christ. This is why we affirm that our identity with God is found in Christ.

I remember wrestling with this concept for the first time as a teenager. When you're sixteen, you identify yourself by your friends, your clothes, your car, and your academic or athletic abilities. I struggled to understand what it meant to find my identity in Christ. It sounded good. It sounded like something that would bring freedom, but I didn't know how to think differently about myself.

When I became a mother, I desperately wanted my children to recognize their unique God-given identity. As I watched my children struggle with this, God began to reveal to me why *my identity* was foundational for the kind of faith that I wanted them to possess. For the first time, I was awakened to the reality of who I believe God created me to be and what plan I believe He has for me to fulfill. This awakening began to shape the way I viewed myself and how I made decisions accordingly.

As an eyewitness to my children's lives, I could see how what they believed about themselves influenced their decisions.

When the world told them they were ugly, annoying, stupid, or unwanted, I wanted to shout out at the top of my lungs, "No, you are not! You are lovely, wanted, and treasured!" It frustrated me that some punk kid down the street had more credibility than I did.

Then I thought about God as *my* Father. I thought about how the world had told me that I was worthless, unloved, and simply not enough—and how I had made decisions accordingly. I sought worth, love, and a life that would prove I was *enough*. Tenderly, God was shouting through Jesus, "You are worth it! You are loved! I am enough!" This was the "Aha" moment that changed everything.

Image Bearers

When we receive God's identity for us (and believe it), we experience freedom. Suddenly the opinions of the world and those around us pale in comparison to the voice of our Father. As we live in our identity, seeking to live out the life we were created to live in Christ, then we can genuinely ask the next question: "Who did God create my *child* to be?" It is here that we begin to understand the Father's heart for spiritual parenting.

This is often a difficult posture for us as parents. We may believe in our minds that our children belong to God and that they were created for His glory, but daily living can tempt us to believe that they were created to reflect *us* instead of the Father. I can remember thinking and even saying to my children, "Don't do that, because I will be embarrassed in front of my friends." In that sentence, I am communicating that my child is a reflection of me and that it is his job to bring me acclaim, or not cause me shame, by his actions. How arrogant of me! Instead, from the beginning, we ought to see our children as image bearers of God for His glory.

Each of us was created in God's image. We bear His fingerprint—and no two are alike. At the end of our season of parenting, don't we ultimately want children who look like Christ? That is a much higher goal than simply trying to keep our children from embarrassing us in public, right?

So how will we accomplish this?

- We must repent from the temptation to create and mold our children into our own image.
- We must die to ourselves and to our personal ambitions for our children and sincerely seek God every day, asking Him to reveal His plan for them.
- We must recognize afresh the larger story line that God is writing—His grand redemptive narrative in which each of us has a part to play. This includes our children. We don't want them to miss out on the unique contribution that God created them to fulfill.

Only when we do these things are we ready to embrace what God has in store for our children. Spiritual parenting gives us the privilege of watching God's plan unfold before our very eyes.

Because God Said So

One of my favorite places to go for encouragement in this endeavor is in the Bible, in Ephesians 1. In beautiful imagery these verses demonstrate what is true about our identity in Christ when we have received Jesus as Savior.

> Praise be to the God and Father of our Lord Jesus Christ, who has *blessed us* in the heavenly realms with every spiritual blessing in Christ. For he *chose us* in him before the creation of the world to be *holy and blameless* in his sight. In love he predestined us to be *adopted as his sons* through Jesus Christ, in accordance with his pleasure and will—to the praise of his glorious grace, which he has freely given us in the One he loves. In him we have redemption through his blood, the forgiveness of sins, in accordance with the riches of God's grace that he lavished on us with all wisdom and understanding....

> In him we were also chosen, having been predestined according to the plan of him who works out everything in conformity with the purpose of his will, in order that we, who were the first to hope in Christ, might be for the praise of his glory. And you also were included in Christ when you heard the word of truth, the gospel of your salvation. Having believed, you were marked in him with a seal, the promised Holy Spirit, who is a deposit guaranteeing our inheritance. (vv. 3–8, 11–14)

I don't know what stood out for you in that. But this passage is filled with markers of our identity in Christ. I'd encourage you to read it again—slowly, digesting every word. Because if we truly began to believe any of it, we would stand a little taller, with our heads a little higher—if we *really* believed it! Think about the provisions that God has made for us, said about us now and in our future, and valued to do in us because of His great love. I think it would impact the way that we lived if we thought those things were true.

It's easy for us to say, "Well, I'm just *one* of seven billion people who are living on this earth right now … and there have been billions who have lived before me; I'm no more than a small drop in the sea of humanity." Unfortunately our children might be feeling this way in our homes, in their schools, or at their churches. Perhaps they feel insignificant and alone.

Nancy Pearcey reminds us, "The Bible does not begin with the Fall but with Creation: Our value and dignity are rooted in the fact that we are created in the image of God, with the high calling of being His representatives on earth. In fact, it is only *because* humans have such high value that sin is so tragic.… [But] He restores us to the high dignity originally endowed at Creation—recovering our true identity and renewing the image of God in us."[9] What if our children were to grasp this identity that is available in Christ? What if this truth were to sink down deep into the bedrock of who they are? This would be life changing, wouldn't it?

Well, guess what? God chose *you* to be the first person who would usher this truth into your child's heart. He has entrusted *you* with the unique privilege of helping your children discover their identity!

Don't Mess with Me!

One day I wrote a statement, based on Ephesians 1, that I thought might help my children to know and understand their true identity. I wanted each of them to be immersed in this truth so that they would know in their core who they were when they were tempted to make a decision that was incongruent. I personalized it for each of my children, and I personalized it for myself as well.

Mine reads, "My name is Michelle Anthony. I am the chosen and adopted daughter of the Most High King. I'm the heir to an eternal inheritance waiting for me in heaven. I have been bought and completely paid for by the perfect sacrifice of Christ's own blood and am sealed throughout all eternity by God's Holy Spirit. Don't mess with me!"

This is the confidence I wanted my kids to have! I wanted these words of truth to run through their heads: I'm a child, I've been bought, I've been chosen, I'm adopted, I'm an heir, and my sin has been completely paid for. All of these things scream freedom! I put this statement on the wall next to their beds, in their Bibles, in their lunches—so that they would remember who they were when the Enemy attempted to seduce them to believe otherwise.

Prowling, Roaring Lion

The Enemy will seduce our children. He will offer them a multitude of counterfeit identities. He will lie to them, deceive them, and rob them of their true identity if he can. He wants nothing more than to destroy them. First Peter 5:8 says, "Your enemy the devil prowls around like a roaring lion looking for someone to devour." As a parent, I want to protect my child at all cost, but I lose sight of *this* Enemy at times. I lose sight that the real Enemy of my children's hearts and souls is a powerful evil that preys on them. With trickery and distortion, he promises everything and gives nothing but pain, regret, and bondage.

It is interesting to me that the apostle Paul begins his letter to the church in Ephesus by proclaiming their identity in Christ and then ends his letter in chapter 6 with the recognition that Satan himself will seek to not only thwart that identity but destroy it.

> Finally, be strong in the Lord and in his mighty power. Put on the full armor of God *so that you can take your stand against the devil's schemes.* For our struggle is not against flesh and blood, but against the rulers, against the authorities, against the powers of this dark world and against the spiritual forces of evil in the heavenly realms. (vv. 10–12)

Paul knew, as assuredly as Christ came to give us His truth and His character, that Satan would come to steal those very things from us. The Bible tells us that our Enemy, the Devil, began his treachery against humanity in the garden by deceiving Eve and that his final act in this world will be when he is unleashed to deceive the nations. His favorite tool is *deception.* Of course I've seen its effect on my own life, but it has pained me to watch his deception affect my children's lives.

The Lie

My husband and I agreed that as we raised our children we would give them incremental opportunities to gain freedom and independence.

We didn't want to withhold all of these opportunities until they were eighteen and then suddenly unleash our children into the world. Finding the balance for each child to gain the confidence needed for adulthood is sometimes a tricky business. We were in constant need of wisdom and guidance to understand each child and to determine when we should put up more boundaries and when we should eliminate a few.

At sixteen, our daughter had a strong desire to stay alone overnight. She wanted to brave it out and build the confidence needed to make her own dinner, lock down the house, take care of the pets, and victoriously awake with the house still standing. It felt like a challenge to her. Of course we had our reservations, but when an overnight retreat, not far away, arose … we decided to give her a chance at it. She had her driver's license if there was an emergency, we had friends nearby, and my son was at a sleepover. We told her she could invite over her two best friends, lock the doors, and watch movies. Sounded like a good plan, right? Wrong!

The next morning we received a phone call from our daughter wondering when we would be coming home. Hmmmmm. This was our independent daughter. Certainly she wasn't *missing* us. With that cue, my husband headed straight to the house. What he found was more than we could have imagined. The remains of what must have been the party of the century led a trail from our front yard to the front door. Inside were three girls shaking with fear and regret. The trash, the stench, the glares from neighbors—all painted a picture of what had transpired in the twelve hours before my husband's arrival. The girls began to cry.

Damage Control

The tale unfolded: Three teenage girls had simply invited a few friends, who invited a few friends, who invited a few friends … and so on. As the list grew, so did the lack of morality. By the time the house was full (and then some), my daughter didn't recognize but a few of the faces. It had gotten so far out of control that she was scared. Just then there was a knock at the door—a friendly visit from the local police department.

What makes this story even more interesting is that my husband serves as the chaplain for the police department. As they entered our home they asked, "Wait, isn't this Chaplain Anthony's home?" Nice! Not exactly the words you want to hear! The police immediately emptied the house and gave our daughter some choice words of correction and wisdom. Then she began to clean and wait for our return.

My husband called me on my way home to prepare me, and so I asked him to put my daughter on the phone. She cried, "I'm sorry, Mommy," a thousand times. I prayed as she lamented on the other end. I really wanted to be a spiritual parent in this. I didn't want to simply punish her (although I had some great ones flowing through my mind). I wanted to *redeem* this moment for her ultimate good. After all, isn't that how God parents us?

The first (and only) thing that came to my mind was that my daughter had forgotten *who* she was. "Certainly she must not be aware of her true identity, or she would have made better decisions," I thought. So I told her that I wanted her to write an essay. I wanted her to entitle it "A 16-year-old Christian Girl." I told her to describe what that person looked like according to God's standards and His

Word. I didn't want to preach at her—I was curious what *she* thought that person looked like.

As I drove home I considered resigning from my position at the church—and as a mother. I was discouraged. What business did I have talking about parenting when clearly I had not instilled an identity of Christ in my own child? I felt like a failure.

When I walked into the house, I was greeted by the stark reality of all that had taken place in our absence. We assessed the damage and the stolen property. We pieced together what had happened and how it had spun out of control. We talked to neighbors. We prayed for wisdom. Then I walked upstairs to my daughter's room, and taped to the door I found these words:

A Sixteen-year-old Christian Girl by Chantel Anthony (age 16)

She should be an example to all of her friends of how Christ would like us to live our lives. She should live for Christ—living out loud, not only just the talk but also walking the walk. The way she talks should not contradict the way she lives. A Christian girl shouldn't feel the pain of guilt but the freedom of truth. She has her priorities in check, God first and others follow behind. She doesn't ignore the Holy Spirit when He knocks at her heart but rather answers it right away. She listens to her conscience and the Holy Spirit because she knows that God knows best.

She stands up against peer pressure and doesn't let the world transform her into something she isn't. She stands strong and sets a good example for others to follow. She is truthful and trustworthy, righteous and obedient. She is light among darkness and is a love song that reflects God in all of His glory. She is open with her beliefs and doesn't care about what others think about her. She acts as Christ Himself would live. She is pure and innocent before Him.

She is trusted by her parents and loved and admired by her friends. She leads her friends to be better rather than allowing her friends and the rest of society to conform her to the world. She finds comfort in the Lord. She leans on Him and calls upon Him in times of trouble instead of trying to figure it out on her own. She is loved and rewarded by God, and He delights in her. She is growing in Spirit and in Christ and acknowledges that every obstacle she is given is thrown her way only to test her and make her stronger.

This sixteen-year-old Christian girl should be me, but I have become too wrapped up in the world to care. I want to change and become this true example of Christ and love song to the world.

I was overwhelmed. I had no idea that all of the things that my husband and I had written on my daughter's heart, for so many years, had actually taken root. She knew them. She desired them. She understood deep spiritual truths that only God could have revealed to her. She could define her identity after all.

She had made a mistake—a big one—and many more would follow. But ultimately, she knew who she was created to be and the God who had created her—and this was quite different from what I had envisioned during my drive home. Obviously there would be course correction and natural consequences, but my heart was filled with joy, because I knew that the work of knowing her identity was deep in her heart. If she knew who she was but was not acting on it, then she had simply *forgotten*.

Forgotten Identity

We all suffer from forgotten identity at times. I know I have! It's a case of spiritual amnesia, and its effects can be debilitating. I knew this was a critical time in her life, and so I continued to ask God what I needed to do next. He was the only one who knew how to parent *this child* in *this situation*. What I did next may seem strange, but I knew almost instantly that I needed to do it.

As we gave my daughter her list of consequences, we also told her to pack her bags. No, we were not sending her away to live with her long-lost aunt (but I confess that I did linger long enough so that she had to consider what might happen next!). Rather, I was taking her on a trip to the mountains. What? To most onlookers this appeared to be a reward, not a consequence. But I knew that she had forgotten who she was and that she needed to spend some time with me. Just the two of us. I prayed that God would help her *remember* by being alone with me away from the distractions of her life.

We swam, we sat on surfboards on the lake and talked for hours, we shopped, I read to her, we ate breakfast by the lake—and slowly I saw "my daughter" emerge again. She was beginning to remember. We came home, and she was refreshed and stronger. She began the next school year with a growing sense of awakened identity that continues to be shaped until this day.

I did not fully appreciate that moment until just a few months ago. It has been three years since that mountain getaway, but my daughter's words in my most recent Mother's Day card read, "I love that you took me to the lake after I threw that party … thank you for swimming, talking, and shopping. Thank you for wanting to be with me." Wow! All this time had passed, and yet she remembered that when she had made a bad decision I didn't *send her away* … but rather I *brought her close*.

God helped me to be a spiritual parent that day. I'm not smart enough to come up with something like that! I didn't know what was deepest inside of her that needed to be healed … or what needed to be done to heal it. Taking away her cell phone or her car can feel like good consequences, but in this case, God wanted to teach her something about Himself. She commented that now when she fails, she doesn't feel the need to hide or run from God. She knows that she can draw close to Him so that she can remember who she is—simply by spending time with Him.

I Choose Truth

The words my daughter penned in her identity statement have challenged me many times. True faith occurs when it permeates the whole of who I am. Then, when I am asked to deny that faith or act incongruently to it, it is almost impossible. This is what Paul was talking about in Ephesians 1. In essence he was saying that once you grasp the magnitude of who you are in Christ, it will affect *everything* else.

The reason it doesn't have this impact is because we often use our faith as an "add-on." It's there for us when it's convenient or when we *feel* like it. When this occurs we rob ourselves of true transformation, because where there is truth with faith there is genuine transformation. True identity gives me the confidence to say to temptation, "Who I am in Christ is something much deeper, much more meaningful, and it is eternal—which is more than this moment, this *very little* moment. So I choose truth instead." Wow! I want that for my children—and I want that for me as well, because I can't give away something that I don't have.

But They Will Fail

I feel like this is the conversation that I have more often than not with my children. The conversation of identity lost. The conversation of redemption. My children will fail. They will choose the lie, and they will take the bait. We have. We do. Think about it.

But spiritual parenting tells our children, "Yes, this time you did not choose truth, but this does not *define* you. This is *not* who you are. This is something you *did*, but it is not *who you are*. You're still the same person. You still belong to God—you are in Christ. And that can't be taken away." We must remind them of their true identity because guilt and shame are debilitating demons.

Max Lucado once said, "Satan [sows] seeds of shame. If he can't seduce you with your sin, he'll let you sink in your guilt. Nothing pleases him more than for you to cower in the corner, embarrassed that you're still dealing with the same old habit. 'God's tired of your struggles,' he whispers. 'Your father is weary of your petitions for forgiveness,' he lies…. [But your] temptation isn't late-breaking news in heaven. Your sin doesn't surprise God."[10]

My husband once used an intriguing metaphor to illustrate this truth. He described a book that had many pages. Most of the pages were white, but many were darkened to varying degrees. As he described one of the dark pages in that book, he noted that it represented failure and sin. He also noted that it was just a page. That one dark page did not define the book, nor did the others that were also scattered throughout. Rather, the book was defined by its title and what was written on the pages themselves.

We all have dark-page moments, even seasons, in our lives. Our children will too. Yet the story is much greater than that. God is bigger than our sin and mistakes, bigger even than the text written on those pages that we would rather forget. Looking back, I see that it is often those very pages that make me even more beautiful as my story of redemption is told in God's grand narrative. When our children fail, we need to remind them of who they are so that they can walk in the confidence of God's grace, which He has lavished upon each of us in Christ Jesus (Eph. 1:7–8).

Our Words Define

Our words carry enormous weight in our children's minds. Our words actually shape their view of themselves in profound ways. To say things such as, "You're so stubborn," or, "You're so negative," or, "You are not a grateful person," creates identity for them, but in the wrong way. Oddly, we tend to make identity statements about the negative aspects of our children. Things such as, "She is shy," or, "He's not very athletic"—instead of giving life to them by saying, "She tends to be quick to listen, taking in her environment," or, "He is gifted in the arts."

Many of us may have had parents who said things about us that we know aren't true, yet we still struggle with them because those words (or lack thereof) marked our hearts when we were young and our identity was forming. Yet we have a heavenly Father who chose to radically burst through our pain, through Christ, and redeem us by His love! We can take this healing that we have received and pass it on to the next generation—we speak these things into their lives. They need to believe these things are true. Part of their journey will be centered on what you and I believe about them. They need to believe that they *are* the person that Christ has identified them to be.

The Blessing

One way we can do this is to offer them a blessing in our words. A blessing is a beautiful gift to give our children. We started blessing our kids at bedtime when they were young, but when they got older and we were not physically putting them to bed anymore, we blessed them before school or as we dropped them off at sports practice. A blessing can be reading Scripture to them, praying it over them, or simply praying truth over your children. It's good to offer a touch as well, affirming your love. Look your child in the eye and say, "Your father loves you," or, "Your mother loves you"—and then pray the passion that you have in your heart for them.

I would bless my son by praying, "Brendon, your mother loves you. I pray a blessing over you to be strong and courageous, to be bold in your faith, to stand up for what you know is right. I believe these things will happen in your life because of the Holy Spirit and the power that is yours in Christ Jesus." This is a unique privilege—to pray over your children, to affirm their identity out loud. Oftentimes we pray in silence for our children, but if we speak a blessing to them faithfully, God can use these spoken words in ways that will bring them confidence in their identity as we give language to the work that God is doing in their lives.

Choosing an Identity

Our children are tempted by counter-identities every day. The question is not whether they will choose one or not, but *which one* they will choose. Spiritual parents take the environment of identity seriously because they understand how much is at stake! If we don't offer them the identity of knowing Christ and being transformed by His Spirit, make no mistake about it: The world will offer them a wide array of choices. This is why Paul urges us to "not conform any longer to the pattern of this world, but be transformed by the renewing of your mind" (Rom. 12:2). Our children's minds are renewed by the truth of God in our lives and in His Word.

It is a normal process for preteens and teenagers to experiment with several identities, much like one trying on different outfits to see which fits best. However, those who have been granted a new identity in Christ are sealed by God's Spirit. He will be faithful to them and continue the work in their hearts for a lifetime. I take comfort in remembering Philippians 1:6: "He who began a good work in you will carry it on to completion until the day of Christ Jesus."

My son recently turned sixteen. Although he may not encounter the same forgotten-identity moment that my daughter did when she was sixteen, I know he will have his own. I pray for his heart, knowing that even though the Enemy is seeking to devour his faith, Jesus is interceding on his behalf every day. He is continuing a work in my daughter, my son, and in me—lest I ever forget that I, too, am a child of God who bears the marks of His identity.

5

Help from Our Friends

The Environment of the Faith Community

The faith of children is most likely to grow when
they have the opportunity to associate with
adults who are growing persons who know
and love God. The child's faith is inspired
when he or she belongs to an inclusive
community that seeks to live out God's love.

Catherine Stonehouse[11]

My Friends Are Waiting

One morning when my son was only four, he plopped himself on my
bed. Carefully he leaned forward to my face and proceeded to gently
open my eyes with his tiny fingers. I heard him whisper, "Don't close
eyes, Mommy." Half-asleep, I said, "Yes, Mommy close eyes," hoping
that he would get the idea and let me have just a few more minutes.

But alas, he did not. "Mommy, today is Sunday, and my friends are waiting for me," he said with such sincerity.

Instantly I was awake. I was surprised that my son knew it was Sunday, wanted to go to church, and understood that there was a community of friends waiting for him. Much to his delight and my satisfaction, we pulled the family together and made our way to the community that had been, for a moment, taken for granted.

No Man Is an Island

We weren't created to live in isolation. We weren't meant to do this thing called the Christian life alone. Without being involved in a vibrant faith community, we can begin to live secluded lives of faith. When this happens, we literally start to forget who we are. As we discussed in chapter 4, our identity has a profound impact on the way we live and the choices we make. What we believe about who we are and where we aim our heart determines the outcome of our lives for eternity. As the battle rages against our identity, the faith community brings us strength.

God designed the faith community to build up each believer for this battle that we face when we leave the security of "family." This faith community offers a support system among people who are like-minded, who believe the same truths, and who ultimately want the same things out of this life. These shared beliefs and values provide a powerful foundation for our children, especially during their developmental years. And as our children grow older, weekends at church or faith-inspired events within a vibrant community of believers give our children a momentary reprieve from the world's pressures and antagonistic jeers.

Christian educators Merton Strommen and Richard Hardel illustrate this point in their book, *Passing on the Faith*: "We live in a time when many families are disintegrating. There will continue to be hurting people, more psychologically scarred youth, more fragmented families in the future of every congregation. Fewer youth will know close family life and the security of being loved and cared for. For them a congregation of faith can provide the experience of being part of a close family."[12]

It's tempting for parents to have the perspective that life has become too busy and cluttered, and therefore having Sundays off is the only time to simply rest. We may have good intentions, but often getting to church can become "just one more thing" in a busy family schedule. Many churches across the United States consider a "regular attendee" someone who goes to church once a month! But that's not remotely enough support for any of us.

Shared Values

When my kids were little, it was difficult for them to experience true community with other believers unless I was diligent to create it. Our kids desperately need the faith community because it is the one place where there are other people who worship the same God, believe the same things, and are dedicated to living the same life. Our children need to know they are not alone.

During my kids' growing-up years, we didn't live near our physical family members, so the faith community became our "family." We took our vacations with people from our church community, spent holidays celebrating with them, and even attended one another's milestones and sporting events. There were times when I would mourn that we didn't live closer to biological family members, but God showed us how to find deep relationships in our spiritual family as well.

Recently, at my daughter's high-school graduation party, I looked around the room and noticed that, of the thirty people celebrating with her, only six were blood related. Each person wrote a blessing of encouragement and affirmed her decision to follow Christ with her life. This community of faith had strengthened her identity during her childhood years and would now have an impact well into her adult years.

Shared Experiences of God

God also designed us to live within the faith community in order to experience Him in ways that can only happen in close proximity to one another. The faith community creates an environment to equip and disciple parents and children, to celebrate God's faithfulness, and to bring a richness of worship through tradition and rituals. All of these things ultimately offer children a strong sense of identity, security, and belonging.

In ancient Jewish culture, children participated in seven festivals every year where they were able to enjoy the faith community in all of its richness. They ate delicious food, learned and joined in on cultural dances, and shared a common experience with people they hadn't seen in perhaps months—cousins, friends, and family members from all over the region. They'd come together to celebrate sometimes for somewhere between seven and ten days!

Those days together in the faith community were rich markers of faith development. It would have been a spiritually shaping experience for children to live in that type of communal expression of worship. Today, we need to be diligent to ensure we're creating an environment that offers this kind of community for our children.

Reprieve from Temptation

Next, the faith community offers a momentary reprieve from the enticements of the world. The apostle Paul explains that the days in which we live are simply evil. He therefore cautions us to be careful in how we live, ensuring that we are making the most of every moment. In Ephesians 5:15–17 he says, "Be very careful, then, how you live—not as unwise but as wise, making the most of every opportunity, because the days are evil. Therefore do not be foolish, but understand what the Lord's will is."

It wouldn't take much to convince us that the days are evil, would it? We see it every day in the news, the stories we hear, the pain we experience and witness. I have friends who have decided to not have children simply because they're terrified of raising them in this world.

But what does God say about how to live in the midst of this evilness? After all, we are here on this earth because He has determined it so. Therefore, He knew we would be raising children in a world that would be hostile to Him. I can't help but think about the Hebrews, God's chosen people, who endured raising their children in a place extremely antagonist toward their faith: Egypt! God's people lived among thousands of false gods. They were forced into living as slaves in a culture that denied the one true God—and did so for 430 years!

Redeeming the Time

So what plan does God offer to us for living in such a situation? He says this in Ephesians 5: "Be wise!" And He says the way to be wise is to make the most of every opportunity—by *redeeming that time*. The original Greek word that is translated in verse 16 as "making the most of" or "redeeming" is *exagorazo*. This word is interesting because it's not used very often in the Bible. It's a grand concept! *Exagorazo* is the word used to describe something that you would buy or purchase in *totality*.

Let me illustrate. When I think about purchasing something, I think of shoes. Now you may think of handbags or golf clubs, or something else that thrills you, but for me, I love shoes. So for example, if I were to go to the shoe store and purchase a pair of shoes, that would be described in Greek by the word *agorazo*. But if I were to go into a shoe store and completely buy out every pair of shoes they had (just think about backing up a truck to the back of the store and dumping *all* the shoes in it), then that would be *exagorazo*. For me, that's like a dream come true. *Exagorazo* all the shoes!

In the Bible, *exagorazo* doesn't have to do with shoes—it has to do with time. This word means to "completely buy out." It's like when the Grinch stole Christmas; he didn't even leave one tiny ornament, right? It's *everything*. So then the question becomes, how do you and I completely buy out time?

Well, first we must understand what kind of time God is referring to. The time referred to in this passage is not time marked by calendars or watches. Paul uses the Greek word *kairos*, which describes an "opportune or ripe season."

Be Wise—The Stakes Are High

Kairos is a specific, opportune time. As parents we must recognize that there's no greater *kairos* moment than childhood for faith development. We are wise when we seize this *kairos*—this opportune, ripe season in their life—to participate as the Holy Spirit propels them toward faith, the right kind of faith. This is the kind of faith that puts conduct into action based on what they say they believe.

In order for us to "buy out" the totality of time that we have with our children for the purpose of faith formation, we must ensure that our home is a place filled with environments that nurture faith and that we have also given our children the privilege of being part of a vibrant faith community of believers. When these two places, home and faith community, work together in harmony, they have lifelong influence. Neither home nor faith community can do it alone, but together they offer the best opportunity for faith to take root into the adult years.

Make no mistake: This *kairos* moment that we've been given is short. And it feels like it's becoming ever shorter. It's tempting to be lulled into believing that we have more time than we do. Someone once said in regards to parenting that "the days are long and the years are short." Isn't that true? The days turn into months, and the months turn into years, and before you know it our children are in middle school and high school, trying on their faith for size, determining what is *their* faith and what is ours. And then, one day they're gone.

Researchers are finding that many of our Christian kids are walking away from their faith as early as middle school and in even larger numbers after they finish high school. As parents we must do something about this, or one day that will be *our* children. We must behave wisely now in order to pass on to them a genuine kind of faith that will breed longevity.

We must recognize with sober thinking that as we raise our children in the very midst of evil, they will begin to bear the markings of this world to some extent. My own children have been marked by this world in ways that sadden me. There are times when I have wanted to cloister them away in order to protect them. I want to keep them from negative influences and provide them with only the influence of my family and other believers. I must be honest to tell you that it has broken my heart to watch the kinds of situations they have been exposed to.

A Snapshot of Reality

I recently had a discussion with my teenage son about a survey conducted by George Barna on the faith of evangelical believers on high-school campuses. Barna asked thousands of students what they thought about faith in God and the Bible. He asked a series of questions such as, "Do you believe that there is absolute truth? Do you believe that God's Word [the Bible] is ultimate truth? Do you believe that Jesus Christ is God? Do you believe that Jesus' death brings salvation from sin? Do you believe that Jesus rose from the dead?" These beliefs are the critical and foundational pieces of our faith.

Most students surveyed said no to one or more of those questions. Based on their answers, Barna determined that there were, on the average, only twelve evangelicals (those who hold all of the above values to be true) on the average high-school campus in America. Only twelve evangelical Christians on every high-school campus in America! I was overwhelmed by that statistic, yet as I've talked to young people I have found that this is often their experience as well.

I asked my son if he thought this statistic was true. He agreed. He shared that while there may be many kids who call themselves

"Christians," when you actually start unpacking what they believe and whether they're willing to live it, you find a different story. He told me he didn't personally know one guy at his school who believed the same as he did.

The Odd Man Out

Soon after this discussion, my son came home shortly after leaving the house to hang out with some friends. I asked him why he had come home so soon. He told me that when eight of his friends had gotten together, seven of them decided to smoke pot. I looked at him and said, "You were the eighth, right?" He slumped down in his chair and said, "Yeah." He was so discouraged. He said, "I'm so frustrated. I'm just … the odd man out … always. It's so ridiculous. I just can't do this anymore."

We started talking about the statistics of Christians on school campuses again. I told him that I knew it must be difficult—to be one of only "twelve" who are willing to believe this faith and live it. As a mom, my first response was to start talking about getting him into a Christian high school or schooling him from home. I started mentioning the Christian schools in the area, asking him what he thought. Suddenly he just looked up at me and said, "Mom, if I go, then there would only be *eleven* on my campus." Wow! I'll never forget that moment. While I may want to take my kids *out of* this world, God continually shows His power in our kids to help them stand firm *in it!*

Not of This World

Certainly there is nothing wrong with Christian or home schooling. I attended a Christian high school and was strengthened through that experience. But some kids will be placed in the public schools, and they will feel very alone. In that moment I was brokenhearted for my son. He was articulating what the apostle Peter describes in 1 Peter 1:17: living our Christian life as aliens and strangers on this earth. We're *aliens*. Think about that. Do we set up our children to truly understand that this is not our world? Because when you're living like an alien as a child (the very time when you want to fit in so much), it's rough.

Remember Shadrach, Meshach, and Abednego? They were three young Hebrew men living as aliens in the evil empire of Babylon. Yet they were unwilling to compromise their faith and worship a golden idol at the king's whim. God provided courage and salvation to these young men in the midst of difficulty (Dan. 3). One thought that strikes me in this biblical narrative is that the young men *had each other*. I wonder if knowing that there were others who felt the same conviction somehow gave them the courage to stand firm—*together*.

Building Intentional Refuge

It's imperative that we put our children in close proximity to the faith community, because the world is hostile toward their faith. They will need a reprieve. They will need a place where they can take the pieces of their armor off and simply remember who they are. A moment where they're not the alien. In this place, they gain strength. We must be wise to understand that our children will bear the marks of the world's harsh conditions, and therefore we must make provisions for a different kind of community. A community of refuge.

I've had to consider in each season of my children's lives what this would look like. As we participated on weekends at church, as they got involved in small life groups during the week, as we rearranged summer plans in order for our kids to go to camp, as we sought to bring mentors and spiritual family into their daily lives, as we considered sacrifices that we would need to make in order for community to happen in our home—all of these things needed to be made our primary focus.

How would we spend our money in order to make these things a priority? One thing we did was choose to go without some luxury that we desired in order to send our kids to camp with our church group. It would have been easy to say that we couldn't afford it at the moment, but because faith community was a value, we set aside a little money each month to make this a priority.

How would we rearrange our home in order that community could occur more naturally? Well, we decided to turn our garage into a youth lounge where anyone could come at any time. We left the doors open, put in a TV and a sofa, stocked a small fridge with food and drinks, and welcomed community into our lives. And boy did they come! We used our guest room for individuals to stay for a season, while they were in transition. These were mature Christian models for our children to live among.

These types of decisions must be made swiftly and with intentionality. The opportune times we have been given will evaporate without us even noticing! Ask yourself right now, "How will I intentionally and strategically set up an environment where my children will be a vital part of a faith community?"

Renewed Strength

Isaiah 40 describes how those who hope in the Lord will mount up with wings like eagles. This word picture of soaring, of being carried by the wind, makes me think of the freedom and perspective we would experience by flying in such a manner—in contrast perhaps to a hummingbird that flutters her wings, toils, strives, and flies so close to the ground that she can't have the bigger perspective on life.

The faith community offers this freedom and perspective to our children. They learn what it means to "hope in the Lord" together with others. They learn what it means to live by faith instead of sight and to gain an eternal perspective. They are prayed for. They learn about God's Word. They experience God Himself—and others are there to testify that the experiences are real. They need all of these things, just like the Old Testament children whose annual feasts offered them strength for the days ahead when they felt alone and depleted of hope. The world acts as a leech on our children's hearts and souls, and none are unscathed by it.

Remember and Celebrate

In Psalm 145:6–7, David encourages us to remember and celebrate God's character and His works:

> They will tell of the power of your awesome works,
>   and I will proclaim your great deeds.
>
> They will celebrate your abundant goodness
>   and joyfully sing of your righteousness.

In addition, we are told to celebrate in community with others who have been called to the same hope in a living God. In Psalm 22:22, David sings,

I will declare your name to *my brothers*;
in the *congregation* I will praise you.

This pattern is evident in Scripture from the very beginning. In Genesis, the great Creator God paused on the seventh day to remember His work and celebrate that "it was good." He established Passover for Israel so that they would remember and celebrate His great work in delivering His people from the bondage of Egypt. The law regarding the Sabbath acknowledged the need for us to suspend our human efforts and focus on the holiness of God together with other believers.

From God's early history with His people, He required celebrations (feasts) to be part of the natural rhythm of Israel's life. And the New Testament record shows that Jesus and the early church kept these celebrations as well. While we are not bound to keep these feasts, knowledge of them enhances our faith. The symbolism in these feasts is rich and in the context of community gives testimony to the character God demonstrated in His work on our behalf. The seven feasts are:

1. The Feast of the Sabbath (Lev. 23:1–3): a perpetual celebration of worship and rest to mark God's finished work first in creation and then in the redemptive work of Christ on the cross.
2. The Feasts of Passover and Unleavened Bread (Lev. 23:4–8): a celebration of God's miraculous deliverance of the Israelites from the bondage of Egypt and His ultimate deliverance of us from the bondage of sin.

3. The Feast of Firstfruits (Lev. 23:9–14): a remembrance of God's abundant provision through the harvests that provided Israel's food.

4. The Feast of Harvest (Lev. 23:15–22): a celebration of God establishing the nation of Israel at Mount Sinai.

5. The Feast of Trumpets (Lev. 23:23–25): a celebration of God's faithfulness to His covenant promise and the future calling to Himself of all who believe in Christ.

6. The Day of Atonement (Lev. 23:26–32): a remembrance of God's righteousness that demands a sacrifice and the ultimate work of atonement completed in Christ.

7. The Feast of Tabernacles (Lev. 23:33–44): a celebration of Israel's wandering in the wilderness and God's blessing to all who remember their wanderings and seek to obey Him.

Community Builds Relationship with God

In this biblical model, the community intentionally stops to gather together and remember specific things God has done—both at home and in their communal times—and to joyfully worship Him because of who He has been, is, and will be. Following this model, many faith communities celebrate advent, Christmas (Christ's incarnation), Lent, Palm Sunday, Good Friday, Easter (Christ's resurrection), Pentecost, and Passover seders, among others.

During these times we proclaim how we have seen God at work in our lives and offer joyful worship in celebration with others who share our convictions. Can you imagine how exhilarating it would be for our faith if we found a way to live out the value of remembering God and choosing a life of celebration?

Our church has begun something in our children's and youth ministries that allows for this communal pause. Every sixth and thirteenth week within a quarter, we have a *Remember and Celebrate* weekend. These weekends are set apart to do just that: remember what God has done and then take time to celebrate. We don't cover new content, but rather we "feast" on special food or treats, play games that help us remember, and share stories of how God is at work. This tradition has become one that we hope will translate far past the children's time in youth ministry. Our prayer is that our students will transfer this posture into daily living and cultivate hearts that remember and celebrate in any context where they find themselves.

I believe God ordained this kind of rhythm because active remembrance cultivates relationship. God wants us to look back and recognize His faithfulness, intense love, and personal interaction with His people individually and as a community. When we pause to remember, we honor our relationship with God—that intimate relationship in which we speak and He listens, He speaks and we respond. Our response is celebration and worship! It simply cannot be contained!

Visitors Welcomed

I want this type of community for my children. I want them to live in this kind of a world, but I also want it to be inclusive, not some Christian club where we hide ourselves from evil. An exclusive community doesn't teach my child how to live *in* the world and not be *of* it; it just teaches them how to hide from it. The faith community is a place to be strengthened, to be known, to remember God, and to celebrate in worship. In order for the faith community to retain its vibrancy, however, it must continually be increasing in new life and authentic transformation.

When my kids made the decision to be baptized, we wanted to share the experience with others who had been participants and eyewitnesses to their lives. For each of their celebrations, we let them be the ones who assembled the guest list. At my son's baptism celebration, we had many friends and neighbors who did not know Jesus personally or belong to a faith community.

We gathered at the beach for my son to be baptized in the ocean. After the baptism we gathered to bless him by speaking words of encouragement to him. Some shared how they had seen God working in his life or had observed special gifts that God had given to him in order to bless others. Some read verses of encouragement, and others prayed for him. It was a meaningful day for my son to hear so many strengthening words by those who know and love him. When it was finished, his grandfather closed in a prayer of blessing.

As we started to gather things together for dinner (our form of a "feast"), one of out neighbors came up to me with tears in her eyes. The number of people from multiple generations who had gathered together to celebrate and support my son overwhelmed her. She commented that it was encouraging to witness such a strong spiritual support guiding a boy of his age. With that, she confessed that she wanted this for her three boys. As we shared, her heart was awakened to the power of God's faith community. Soon after, she attended church with us, and she and her children came to faith in

Christ. That was eight years ago now, and this friend of mine remains a strong follower of Christ.

I'm often struck by how we as believers try to "package" our faith in ways that might make those not familiar with it feel as if it is "just like their world," only better. We may water it down or compromise our beliefs. Yet that day I realized how much my friend and my children's friends are hungering for something other than what they already have. When we invite them into the faith community in benevolent and gracious ways, they have the privilege to taste and see how good our God is—and how good His community of refuge and celebration is for our souls.

6

What Needs to Be Done?

The Environment of Service

I will often be able to serve another simply as an act of love and righteousness.... But I may also serve another to train myself away from arrogance, possessiveness, envy, resentment, or covetousness. In that case, my service is undertaken as a discipline for the spiritual life.

Dallas Willard[13]

Life As a Chore

God's story, our identity in Him, the community of those who love Him—all of these feed our children's hungry souls. But if their lives are all about intake, they'll grow up to be flabby Christians. That's why even small children need to discover that part of responding to God's love for us is serving Him.

We all had chores growing up, right? I mean, every good home has some form of them. Let's face it, chores were a way to get things done and to help our parents out, but ultimately they were also a way for us as kids to learn to serve the other members in our family—at least in theory. Then why, I wonder, have we for so many decades called this act of service a chore? Think about the word *chore*. It just sounds like a word that makes you want to moan. And we did, didn't we? When my parents told me I could play *after* I finished doing the laundry or the dishes, I simply wailed. I grumbled. I bargained. Anything but a *chore!*

So when I became a parent, I had visions of children who would scurry about in joy, much like Cinderella's mice, knowing that the work just needed to be done. I envisioned them wanting to help out of the abundant gratitude in their hearts for all that we had provided for them. Well, it didn't take long for that dream to be squelched. Innate in each of us is a bent toward selfishness. Instinctively, we know how to serve ourselves and eliminate all else from distracting us in this pursuit. We are not born servants.

Most of us (if not all of us) just naturally come into this world saying, "Serve me." We don't naturally seek to serve others. We are self-centered. We're completely immersed with our needs from infancy. Training a child's heart toward service is counterintuitive to who they are as human beings. But you can cultivate an outward focus in your home by training this posture of the heart, from an early age, through the environment of service.

What Needs to Be Done?

The first three environments discussed in this book focus on creating a big-picture identity for our children. Understanding God's big plan for redemption, internalizing how He has given each of us an identity in Christ to be part of His family, and being with those who are pursuing a relationship with Christ in the faith community—these are all part of establishing a firm foundation in our children's hearts. However, if we stop there, which is tempting to do, we miss out on *why* that foundation was to be built in the first place. This foundation of security and identity allows our kids to begin to look outward, to look toward the interests of others.

Creating an environment where your children from the earliest days ask a very important question is critical for their faith development. The critical question that service asks is simply, "What needs to be done?" This is one of the best questions you can teach your children to ask. To have them walk into any room, situation, or relationship and ask this will change the way they see their world. It's simple. It's profound. Yet this is a posture that will *not* naturally be cultivated in your children unless you set out on an intentional course, making it a priority.

I have seen firsthand, how this simple question has *ruined* my life—in a good way. I am haunted by this question in every corner of my psyche in every situation. It's now so ingrained in me that there are times when I wish I could turn it off, but I can't. As I ask this question, I am most always compelled to respond. Sometimes my response requires great personal sacrifice, and at other times I offer a prayer or find someone else who can respond, but rarely does it let me off the hook completely.

Acts of Service

In my home we chose not to have chores. You're probably thinking, "Wow, your kids must have enjoyed that!" Well, actually we still implemented the concept, but instead of referring to them as chores (which they would see as something to "get done and out of the way") we decided to call them *acts of service*. This might sound silly to you to think that we merely changed the name, but I wanted them to understand that what they were really doing was serving our family.

They needed not only to do what was required for daily living in our home, but also to ask above that, "What needs to be done? We live here in this home. We're participants in this family. What else needs to be done?" So we assigned designated areas of service to our children. My daughter had cleaning bathrooms, doing laundry, and washing dishes every other day, while my son had taking out the trash, mowing the grass, cleaning the spa, and washing dishes every other day. They needed to help with the groceries, the kitchen, the dog, the litter box, and their rooms, as needed. But I didn't want them to think of those things as a list to complete; rather, I wanted them to see our family as interdependent.

I remember the morning when I knew the idea was taking root. Around 6:30 a.m., I heard my son shouting in the hallway before school. Now, my son is not by nature a person who shouts or is easily upset, but that morning he was. As I lay in my bed I heard these words resonate through our upstairs hallway: "Mom! Chantel has not done her *act of service,* and now I have no underwear for school." Although I then heard the argument that ensued as my daughter suggested that *he* was capable enough to wash his *own* underwear, I snuggled down in my bed with the satisfaction of knowing that not only had my son referred to the laundry as an act of service at 6:30 a.m., but that they had both seen how dependent we were upon each other for our needs to be met.

Have You Served Your Family Today?

In this model, while we all have our customary tasks, we *also* live in a home that asks, "What needs to be done?" So if my son sees that there is a huge pile of laundry, he can put in a load of whites on any given day. My daughter is free to serve our family by picking up groceries and making dinner one night if I am asked to stay later at work. We seek to do this for each other because that is what needs to be done—we don't want to simply live life by checking off our own personal list of duties.

It's a great reminder to ask one another at dinner, "How did you serve your family today?" On the occasion that your family has served one another, this will be a time of gratitude. On the occasion that your family has been more self-serving, this will be an opportunity to remind one another of the ways that you need the other members of the family. Perhaps after sharing, your family can pray that they will not only be sensitive to ways they can serve in the future, but that God will give them the strength to be selfless and generous with their time and energy.

I know one family that has a whiteboard next to their front door. As they enter and exit, they see the names of their family members. As they seek to serve their family, they simply sign their initials next to the name of the member they served in some way. It doesn't say *what* was done, but it offers visual accountability to each member of the family to fulfill what the apostle Paul wrote in the same chapter where he connected worship with service (Romans 12).

He said, "Be devoted to one another in brotherly love. Honor one another above yourselves. Never be lacking in zeal, but keep your spiritual fervor, serving the Lord" (Rom. 12:10–11). Ultimately, when we serve each other, we are serving the Lord.

Cinderella's Mice?

Now let me make one thing clear: My children are not always smiling, dancing, and joyfully running through our house doing acts of service at all times, like the mice in *Cinderella*. The reality is that my children give me tremendous pushback about serving our family, just as I am sure yours will. But as spiritual parents we are choosing to live this way because it's a daily reminder to them of what their true calling is—not only in our home but in life. This is their calling from God.

We model at home what it looks like to live in this world as Christ-followers. So, if we have *chores* at home in a place that's supposed to be a testing ground for all of life, then they may see serving others as an obligatory chore when they're out in the world. Something to check off of their list. They may see situations of need as "not their job" or rationalize that they already "did their job." Will they respond, "I didn't make that mess," or will they see each circumstance as an opportunity to simply serve someone else?

God has designed us to live interdependently in this world. As Paul writes in Philippians 2:3–4, "Do nothing out of selfish ambition or vain conceit, but in humility consider others better than yourselves. Each of you should look not only to your own interests, but also to the interests of others."

The Attention It Deserves

We begin by training our children that God has asked us, as His children, to be servants. We train them with this knowledge, and then we model it by *calling it out* every time we do it. If we serve at church or in our neighborhood, we tell them *why* we are serving.

By explaining why I am doing something, I am able to tell my children, "I asked the question, 'What needs to be done?' and then I realized that I was needed to do this." Or, "I'm here at church and we're setting up chairs because I asked the question, 'What needs to be done?' and chairs needed to be set up." Or, "I'm cleaning up trash in McDonald's right now because someone left a mess, and I asked the question, 'What needs to be done?'" We reinforce this heart posture through repetition. We tell and show our children in every situation what it means to be a servant.

So often we're great models of service, but our children don't know *what* we're doing or *why* we're doing it. In order to bring clarity to this, we must call attention to it. This is not the same as bragging about your actions. It is instructing your children what true service is. As your children get older you won't need to say it as much. They'll be saying it. Children who have been raised in this environment are evident. They walk into any situation, and they go straight to what needs to be done. It's a posture of their heart and of their spirit.

My Own Selfishness

I must confess that as a parent I don't always model this. Too often I model the opposite. I enter a situation where something is needed, and I feel the urge to take care only of myself. I find myself rationalizing how busy I am, how tired I am, or how much I have already given of myself. I have the time, the energy, and the ability, but I just sit drinking my latte, wondering why things aren't being done "better."

We first have to recognize our own bent and that we are not serving in the most basic of ways. When we do, we will better understand why it's hard to give this type of heart to our children. It's difficult, even impossible, to give away something we don't already have.

In order to give this gift to our children, we must become servants, and then our children will see our faith in action. As we walk into situations, even this week, whether it's in our homes, our workplaces, our neighborhoods, our churches, our communities—wherever it is, we can start by asking ourselves, "What needs to be done?" As you do this, look around you. You will discover how different things appear.

A Serving Experience

Recently we offered a "serve experience" for our families at our church. We put together individual packets for our families so they could have their own "What needs to be done?" experience. As each family participated in the elements included in the packet, they were guided through reading Scripture, praying, and then driving in their cars or walking through their neighborhoods.

I thought about myself—how many times had I jumped in my car simply with a destination in mind? Almost *every* time. Very seldom do people say, "Hey, let's just go for a drive." That sounds like something from the 1950s. Just to *go for a drive* is almost unheard of these days. We use transportation as a means to get *somewhere*.

When we live simply as "destination people," we're not able to ask, "What needs to be done?" Instead, we're asking, "How quickly can I get there?" or, "Who is getting in my way?" because we're probably late and stressed out. Unfortunately, when I do this, I miss out on all the things in between.

It's this "in between" that I wanted for my families in the drive that we asked of them. It allowed them to drive quietly for about fifteen minutes around their community and ask, "What needs to be done?" For me, this was an intriguing thought. I've lived in my own community for almost ten years now. Never once have I driven around for fifteen minutes and asked the question of what needed to be done. Further, I wanted to take my staff at church through this experience to see how it would work before we presented it to our families. They were my guinea pigs.

The Test Run

I sent my staff out into our community in little "family pods." My high-school worship leader was "dad" and I was "mom" in one car, along with "our kids"—one administrative associate and one children's associate. We had fun as we drove off, watching our kids in the back, who were throwing things at each other and shouting, "He's touching me," and all the things we supposed a family would have to endure on their journey of exploration.

We stopped to read the verses, to pray, and to get ready to ask our question of what needed to be done in our neighborhood. We were so eager to serve. We first found an empty lot that had trash, so we jumped out and started cleaning it. We saw a homeless man, and we gave him a sandwich. We went to a park and cleaned bathrooms. We saw a woman carrying groceries to her car, but when we started to approach her, she ran away! Funny. Overall, we were feeling good about it, but we were also thinking about what God might still have in store for us in this.

We drove past a little café. I had been there only once, but I remembered the owner, an older woman who worked very hard to keep it going. I wanted to stop and just say hi to her. We prayed, "Lord, here's a woman, here's a café, what needs to be done?" So we walked in and asked her if there was anything we could do for her. We mentioned that we could clean her bathrooms or wash her dishes. She just looked at us as if we were insane. At first she asked if we were in need of a free meal or something. She spoke in broken English with a beautiful Spanish cadence.

In my best Spanglish, I tried to say, "We just came to serve you. We figured that this would be a busy time for you. It's right after lunch. You probably have a lot of dishes." She smiled—and with that she handed us a mop, a towel, and some soap. Off my "family" went, serving. Two of us went into the kitchen and started washing dishes. The other two got mops and gloves and started cleaning toilets and bathrooms. Finally, she came up to me and asked, "Tell me, *why* are you here?"

Messengers of Hope

I told her that we worked at the church a couple of doors down and that we were asking God to send us where we could go and be of service in our community today. And we felt like God just led us over here to be with her. The woman burst into tears. She began to share her story: "I'm a single mom, and it has always been my dream to own my own restaurant, but it hasn't been going well, and in fact, the landlord is coming in *today* to get the keys from me. Today is my last day."

She continued, "I woke up this morning, and I started praying. I haven't prayed in many years. I was crying out to God that I needed to have some hope, and I asked Him, would He please send an angel or a messenger? Would He send some message of hope to me so that I would know that He still cared?" And then she looked at us and said, "You're my angels."

We started praying for her. We told her this was not the end. We reminded her that, although it might be the end of this particular dream, God had something else planned for her. We told her that we believed God did send us to her that day to encourage her to return to Him and to trust Him alone. We hugged her. We recited Scripture to her, and then we left.

I drove by the café the next day, and she indeed was gone. The doors were closed. But we were able to be messengers of God, of love, of hope, and of service to this woman who desperately needed it, because we simply asked the question, "What needs to be done?"

Sometimes we are privileged to see the end result of these stories and hear the blessings. And sometimes we do acts of service in quiet, where no one sees, and only God knows the eternal impact that we're making. It's necessary to train our children that sometimes we're going to see the result and sometimes we don't, but either way, it's an act of spiritual service to God. Service is our act of worship to Him. We're serving Him by serving others. When we serve Him, we're obedient. Eternal things happen. Lives are changed.

Faith Alive

Remember from chapter 2—faith without works is dead, right? What is the work of faith then? I desire "live" faith, and I desire for my kids to have live faith as well. The work of faith is *action.* Jesus commands us to put our faith into action. I've had the honor of watching young people do this. It's compelling to see how even little ones understand that putting their faith into action is life-giving for them—it makes God a reality to them. In some way it helps all these things we ask them to do make sense. And one of the ways we help produce active faith in our children is by serving.

One thing I do not want to do as a parent is just continue to fill my children's brains with lots of information about Scripture and God but then not give them opportunities for expression. As parents, one of our roles is to match the experiences of faith and action with the knowledge that they're learning. We need to be intentional about this. We will always fight the temptation to make our children into cognitive Christians.

When my children were little, I took pride in the fact that they could recite the books of the Bible and many Bible verses, and if I was telling a Bible story that they could name the main characters. We even spent time learning the names of all twelve disciples. (Try it—it's not that easy!) At family get-togethers, I would have our children perform, and family members of all ages thought I was a good mom for this. Until it was bedtime, of course, and I couldn't get my son to stay in his bed! Then the eyebrows began lifting.

The Milk Diet

Now these are wonderful tools and certainly a great foundation for our children, but often we stop with the elementary levels of learning: memorization, behavior modification, and moral instruction. Somewhere along the way, we forget to wean them from this milk and into a diet of solid food. The solid food is faith not measured by what we *know* but by how we put what we know into *experience*. Righteousness is the act of aligning our actions to our love for a holy God.

The writer of Hebrews addresses this very thing:

> We have much to say about this, but it is hard
> to explain because you are slow to learn. In fact,
> though by this time you ought to be teachers, you
> need someone to teach you the elementary truths
> of God's word all over again. You need milk, not
> solid food! Anyone who lives on milk, being still
> an infant, is not acquainted with the teaching
> about righteousness. (5:11–13)

The Epic Adventure

Part of "the teaching about righteousness" is that faith is a muscle that has to be used. I have seen children whose faith is really strong, but if they don't use it, that muscle becomes deteriorated over time. What often happens is that by the time our children are in high school, their spiritual muscles are wimpy and weak, when in reality they should be storming the world with their faith. Their muscles have atrophied so much because we've not entrusted to them the things of faith.

One of those things is a servant's heart, of course, but serving in a prepackaged way is *milk*. It is important that we give our children ways to serve that we have determined for them when they are young. However, as they get older, we must progressively take away the packaging and allow them to put their faith into action without our guardrails.

Instead of saying to our preteens and teens, "You need to show up on this day, at this time, and bring this amount of money … and then you'll be able to put your faith into action," we need to let them depend on God's Spirit to tell them as *they* ask the question for themselves.

After all, how *epic* is it to tell our students that we have nicely packaged their faith in action? How compelling is that for a teenager? Really, that kind of service just seems like any other field trip they're going on. And quite frankly it probably will pale in comparison to a lot of the experiences that they're having in the world or at school.

Instead, the epic faith in action recorded in Hebrews 11, just a few chapters after the charge to long for solid food, is full of radical accounts of living and dying:

> And what more shall I say? I do not have time
> to tell about Gideon, Barak, Samson, Jephthah,
> David, Samuel and the prophets, who through
> faith conquered kingdoms, administered
> justice, and gained what was promised; who
> shut the mouths of lions, quenched the fury of
> the flames, and escaped the edge of the sword;
> whose weakness was turned to strength; and
> who became powerful in battle and routed
> foreign armies. Women received back their
> dead, raised to life again. Others were tortured
> and refused to be released, so that they might

gain a better resurrection. Some faced jeers and flogging, while still others were chained and put in prison. They were stoned; they were sawed in two; they were put to death by the sword. They went about in sheepskins and goatskins, destitute, persecuted and mistreated—*the world was not worthy of them.* They wandered in deserts and mountains, and in caves and holes in the ground. These were all commended for their faith, yet none of them received what had been promised. God had planned something better for us so that only together with us would they be made perfect. (vv. 32–40)

A World Not Worthy

The people whose lives are recounted in this passage are people I admire greatly. They amaze me. They shame me. Sawed in half? Destitute? The world was not worthy of them? They didn't just show up this way overnight. As we read their stories, we see that they were repeatedly using their spiritual muscles. They were dying to themselves daily. They were constantly looking to serve God and others. All of these were manifestations of their faith, and now they inspire us, even though we have not met them.

When I think of "What needs to be done?" I think of how my children and this generation need something epic to live for. They need a cause and an understanding of who God is and what His kingdom is all about. In order to be prepared to be part of such an epic battle, our children will need the environment of service to train their hearts upward and outward. Without it, this generation will settle for something far less than what God has called them to. They will settle for the fruit of selfishness—the vanity of the mundane.

Service as Worship

The early church couldn't even think of worship outside of this concept of service. The Greek word for worship is *latria*. This happens to be the same word for service. *Latria* is service. *Latria* is worship. So the New International Version renders Romans 12:1 like this: "Therefore, I urge you, brothers, in view of God's mercy, to offer your bodies as living sacrifices, holy and pleasing to God—this is your spiritual act of *worship*." The original Greek text can also be translated, "This is your spiritual act of *service*." The two are inseparable. It's the same word. So for us to be worshippers with our lives, we must learn to be servants as well. We must enter into every situation and ask the question, "What needs to be done?"

Preceded by Self-Denial

Service takes a tremendous amount of self-denial, and self-denial is incredibly difficult for us. Yet this is the very foundation of our faith. Mark quotes Jesus saying, "If anyone would come after me, he must *deny himself* and take up his cross and follow me. For whoever wants to save his life will lose it, but whoever loses his life for me and for the gospel will save it" (Mark 8:34–35). While the cross represents death, Jesus so lovingly speaks of it as preceded by self-denial. He notes that if anyone wants to follow Him, then he must first deny himself before he can take up his cross and follow. Self-denial always comes before death. And the journey of a believer is the death of self.

When you create the environment of service in your home and a heart of service toward the world, you establish a path for your children to embrace the cross, and a relationship with Christ, through self-denial.

I encourage you to start today. Ask the question afresh: "What needs to be done?" Cultivate this environment in your home. Ask God to reignite a right perspective in your own heart and mind. Then live it out loud, together as a family, for the glory that will be His in it.

Self-denial for God's glory sounds risky—and it is! So if something in you pulls back from the idea of letting your children take risks in service to God, you've got your toe in the water of the next environment: out of the comfort zone.

7

A Heart of Dependence

The Environment of
Out of the Comfort Zone

Life is comfortable when you separate yourself
from people who are different from you.... But
God doesn't call us to be comfortable. He
calls us to trust Him so completely that we are
unafraid to put ourselves in situations where we
will be in trouble if He doesn't come through.

Francis Chan[14]

Protecting Our Children

I have a friend named Josh who faithfully prays over his three-year-
old son. He often prays for his son to be made into a strong and
courageous man. He asks God to make him mighty and use him for

the sake of Christ. One night while he was holding his son and praying these words, he felt as if God said, "If you're serious about this
prayer, then I'm going to have to hurt him." Now these are not words
that you expect to hear from God, so instinctively Josh pulled his son
in tighter as if to say no. With that, he felt that God responded, "So
you're going to try to protect him from *Me?*"

Wow! What a strong realization that must have been for a young
father! To realize that in order for his son to become the mighty
man he desired, God would have to let his son suffer. And at the
same time to realize that God is our protector and the perfect parent,
because He is willing to do this when we are not.

This story frames the environment of out of the comfort zone.
This young father innately desired to protect, love, and offer comfort
to his son. We are not taught this as parents; we simply react and
respond this way from the first time we hear our infant cry. We are
wired to bring resolution to their pain in any way we can.

However, this environment exposes our children to circumstances and experiences that take them away from their ultimate
places of comfort. In this, children discover that they can no longer
rely upon their own strength and securities (or even ours), so they
begin to learn to depend on God for His strength.

This makes me think of Paul's words when he realizes, "That is
why, for Christ's sake, I delight in weaknesses, in insults, in hardships,
in persecutions, in difficulties. *For when I am weak, then I am strong*"
(2 Cor. 12:10). Here Paul is describing how God uses uncomfortable
situations and trials to accomplish the work He wants to do in us.
Paul recognized that God wasn't trying to be mean-spirited toward
him, but rather that He was using these trials to help him grow in

righteousness. And righteousness is true strength, not the strength that the world promises through our comfort!

Parents to the Rescue!

As a parent, I am intrigued to think about what God's intentional plan is for my child. Let's face it, I have no idea what my children will be someday, who they will influence, or the kinds of things they will be involved in that will build the kingdom of God. But God does. Psalm 139:16 says, "All the days ordained for me were written in your book before one of them came to be."

He knows and understands my children and their individual futures far beyond what I could ever anticipate. I don't know about you, but I don't want to get in the way of that! Instead, I want to align with that plan, much like a sailor putting up a sail to the wind, and come alongside what God is doing in my child's life. I desire to help my child navigate through the trials and uncomfortable places, in order to build his faith muscles, rather than play the part of a rescuer.

As a mom, I was tempted to rescue my children when they were younger. When I heard about so-and-so who bullied my daughter or lied about my son to malign his character, I became infuriated. Immediately I wanted revenge—and this type of "justice" usually meant hurting the child (or the child's parent) who had hurt my child. Okay, maybe not actually *hurting* them, but I did consider how it would *feel* to have him or her brought to justice in some way. I found myself reacting instead of responding. I would take on a posture that said, "I'm going to protect my child at any cost," when really protection is not what they needed most.

Faith Muscles

What my children needed were the skills and faith muscles to be able to walk through the trial and be strengthened, not victimized, by it. This is an essential life lesson for them, *and* it's necessary for me, because protecting my children from the evils of this world would be a full-time job. We live in an evil world. Bad things will happen to our children. People will hurt them intentionally and unintentionally. Life will not be fair.

The best gift we can give our children is the confidence to see that we believe everything is filtered (even the bad stuff) through God's hands. We need to release our control of their circumstances. We need to start looking at these hard things that happen in our kids' lives as things that God wants to use *to refine them*—and then we need to walk with them, prayerfully, and model for them how they should respond in grace under trial.

So take a moment to look at the way you parent. Are you creating an unrealistic place of comfort in your home and in your child's life because of your own fears? Do you rescue your child out of any imperfect situation, friendship, or assignment that might cause your child to suffer? As a spiritual parent, you will need to make this honest assessment. Next, you will need to determine where things are just a little too comfortable or life is just a little too easy, and then begin to think about the practical ways that you can allow trials and suffering to strengthen your children, instead of seeing those things as merely negative.

In Comfort before Out of It

While this environment is of critical importance to our children, it is also essential to remember that one needs a comfort zone to come *out of* before this environment is most effective. You may have no comfort in your life right now. You might be going through divorce, dealing with the illness of a child or a parent, or experiencing an extreme financial difficulty. You may be in one of the millions of homes across the nation where children are being raised amid alcoholism, compulsive spending, mental illness, depression, or anger and rage, just to name a few issues. Many children's lives are in complete upheaval. In these kinds of circumstances life is not comfortable at all.

Some of these are not issues we can control, while others are matters of sin or poor decisions that we have made along the way. The ones we can't control are the ones we must choose to trust that our God is using for our good and His glory. (Of course, these words are easier said than experienced.)

During enormous trial we are burdened, we lack energy and joy, and our focus can become derailed without warning. This is a time where we need the faith community to come alongside us (and our children) in tangible and practical ways. Things like having our children over for a play date or bringing a meal at dinnertime can ease the strain of a difficult season of pain. So if we're in such a season, we may need to intentionally pursue the environment of the faith community more than we have been doing.

In families suffering from the sinful choices of one or both parents, the children are innocent victims. In these situations it is essential that the parents seek the best interest of the children and choose to get help. Many churches and other organizations offer counseling and recovery programs that deal with the specifics of the issues that injure innocent family members.

Perhaps you are an adult victim living with the scars from your childhood and are at risk of repeating those offenses against your own children. Whatever the case, those in recovery ministries say that although we can't choose yesterday, we can always choose today. If your home is not a safe place for your children, choose today to get the help that you need in order to bring security and peace to your children.

Not Enough Comfort … or Too Much?

You will need to assess where your family is right now. What is the climate of comfort in your home? What causes have led you to your comfort or discomfort? If your home has become excessively comfortable because of overprotection and hovering parents, you will recognize the symptoms.

Signs of a home whose children are living in excessive comfort include laziness, ingratitude, lack of motivation, selfishness, entitlement, a critical spirit, and gluttony—among others. When you see the buds of these beginning to blossom, you will know that it is time for the environment of out of the comfort zone. You will want to act—without delay!

There's a New Sheriff in Town

I can remember one day when I had this exact "Aha" moment for myself. I had been gone for most of the day and returned home to a house where dishes were in the sink, the animals were not fed, the TV was blaring in a room with no spectators, trash cans were in the street, food was spoiling on the counter, and a pile of laundry sat in the hallway (so large that passersby must have literally had to step over it dozens of times).

I walked through the house in wonderment, seeking the off-spring of my womb. When I found them, I was shocked to find that they were alive and breathing. Certainly, they couldn't have noticed the messes and needs and not have done anything about it! I wanted desperately to think that they had been abducted by aliens rather than that they would have let me come home to this disaster!

When I showed signs of discontent, they rolled their eyes (always a winner) and moaned, "This is our day off!" I think they regretted that statement later because of the verbal discourse they received on how I never had a day off and how I expected them to serve our family in tangible ways *every day*. Looking back, I see I was upset with them, but more, I was upset with myself.

Truthfully, I had set up this ecosystem by *my* behavior. I had lost sight of the goal and had become slack in my zeal to produce industrious children. It didn't happen overnight, but slowly I had taken over more and more of the responsibilities in my home and had offered my children a huge portion of comfort in every way.

"Are you full, warm, happy, secure, and rested?" are necessary questions to ask an infant, and when we fulfill those things, they smile and nap. But it doesn't work that way for older children and teens! If we do that, they demand more. They become entitled and insensitive, lazy and indignant—and all of this with a bad attitude. Delightful.

In that moment I began to feel empowered. I thought, "Well, then—now there's a new sheriff in town, and things are about to get a little rough around here." With that, I went to work on correcting this place of abnormal comfort that I had created. It didn't happen overnight, and my kids cried out, much like an unused muscle does on the first day of workout, but in time I saw that taking them out of their places of comfort began to produce in them the qualities that had been lacking.

The By-product of Trials

All families will most likely go through seasons of difficulties as well as seasons of prosperity and comfort. In those times of comfort there is a tendency for us to become apathetic in our faith, right? It's ironic, but history tells us that some of the greatest growth periods in the church were during times of tremendous trials and suffering. James explains this correlation:

> Consider it pure joy, my brothers, whenever you face
> trials of many kinds, because you know that the test-
> ing of your faith develops perseverance. Perseverance
> must finish its work so that you may be mature and
> complete, not lacking anything. (James 1:2–4)

For James to even consider that difficult circumstances could be "all joy," he must have highly valued the by-products of such tri-als—perseverance and mature faith.

A few years ago I witnessed a good friend go through a tremen-dous trial. As I watched her, she seemed to have this sense of acute worship about her—an acute prayer life, acute time in God's Word, and an acute sensitivity to the Spirit. I actually said to her, "I'm somewhat jealous of the season that you're in."

Now this was probably not the most sensitive thing I could have said to my friend. I mean, here she was looking for a little comfort, a little understanding, and maybe a little compassion. She was probably looking for me to feel sorry for her and say, "Boy, am I ever glad I'm not going through *that!*" She must have thought that it was really strange or even insensitive of me to say what I did, because I knew she was going through a terrible trial.

But in actuality, I wasn't envious of her trial. I was envious of the by-product of that trial. She was experiencing God—and I wanted that. Of course, I wanted the shortcut version of it. I still do. I want the sunny path, with the glass of lemonade in my hand, as I stroll down the garden trails of experiencing God. I don't want the dark and gloomy road with sharp turns engulfed in deep pits with ragged edges. I want God *and* I want comfort. Trials? No, thank you. And I certainly don't want them for my children, either!

A Time of Distress

Shortly after saying that, God took me through one of the darkest trials of my life (be careful what you ask for). It lasted for a couple of years. In the beginning there was pain, hurt, and betrayal—followed shortly by depression. Then there came depression's friends: bitterness and entitlement.

When I think of those days, I remember thinking it was odd that people laughed out loud in my presence. Didn't they know I was suffering? How insensitive! I am a person who loves to smile, but there were times when I needed to remind myself to smile when in public settings so that I would not offend someone. But the reality was, I had lost my smile. I was far out of my comfort zone, and I didn't like it at all.

One day I envisioned myself standing in a room. I was unclothed. Inside I was full of shame and desperately wanted to dress myself. As I looked down, there were articles of clothing that were within arm's reach. They called out to me to put them on. They promised comfort. These articles had words on them—I could see clearly their names as I rummaged through each one: Anger, Guilt, Bitterness, Entitlement, Jealousy, Pride, and Revenge.

In the distance were other articles of clothing: Kindness, Gentleness, Mercy, Forgiveness, Compassion, Love, Humility, and Peace. I couldn't reach these. I knew instinctively that if these were articles of clothing I would ever wear, then God would have to be the one to clothe me with them, because it was impossible for me to reach them. So I waited. It was painful. I was definitely not in my comfort zone.

Every day I was tempted to clothe myself. To be perfectly honest, there were days when I did try on a few of those outfits—and they brought nothing but more pain. In time, however, He did clothe me. The words of James became true. I watched my faith grow in ways that have permanently marked the person I am today. I do look back with joy, knowing how my relationship in Christ grew deeper. And I have come to understand dependence upon Him in ways I couldn't have known otherwise.

What Am I Afraid Of?

If I know that spiritual growth comes out of my painful trials, why do I try to protect my children from similar experiences? That's the real question. Why would I want to keep my children from the very things that I know, firsthand, will grow their faith in God and their dependence on Christ? Why? Because it pains me to see them hurt. As parents we lose sight of the end goal, and we sacrifice it for today's pleasure. It is counterintuitive to our primal instincts as moms and dads to let our children hurt. But that doesn't mean we shouldn't fight this instinct.

What are we afraid of, anyway? That the pain may be so severe, we won't be able to endure watching it? That they may have such a severe trial, they will lose their faith altogether or wander away from God? Are we afraid that during their trials others may look at us and wrongly judge our parenting skills?

Let's look at each of these things: pain, fear, and pride. They all have one thing in common. These are *my* issues. That's why spiritual parenting is about the kind of person I am as a parent. These are things that I need to confess outright when I see them begin to reveal themselves. I need to take responsibility for the root causes of why I sometimes sabotage this environment in my home.

God Has a Plan

It is in God's nature to create specific and unique circumstances to refine His children. He loves this environment—that's one of the reasons we sometimes have a hard time trusting Him. We say, "If God is all-powerful, then why doesn't He prevent the painful things from happening to me?"

During a trial, I am often tempted to erroneously conclude either that I am not truly His child or that He just loves other people more than He loves me. I do this out of my own dysfunction as a parent. I think of a perfect and loving parent as someone who brings comfort. Instead, a truly perfect and loving parent does the hard stuff and has the ultimate good of the child in mind at all times—no matter what is at stake.

Jesus led His disciples in this manner. He constantly brought circumstances into their lives that He knew would encourage and increase their faith. I don't know if the disciples rolled their eyes— probably not—but I'm sure they weren't always jumping up and down with excitement on days when Jesus said to them such things as:

- "But I tell you: Love your enemies and pray for those who persecute you" (Matt. 5:44).
- "I am sending you out like sheep among wolves" (Matt. 10:16).
- "All men will hate you because of me" (Matt. 10:22).
- "If anyone would come after me, he must deny himself and take up his cross and follow me" (Mark 8:34).
- "Blessed are you when men hate you, when they exclude you and insult you and reject your name as evil, because of the Son of Man" (Luke 6:22).
- "They will put you out of the synagogue; in fact, a time is coming when anyone who kills you will think he is offering a service to God" (John 16:2).

I assume that these were very uncomfortable things for them to hear, but as those who have come to know God's character, we know they came from a place of love.

An Uncomfortable Night to Say the Least

One day, according to Matthew 14, Jesus put His disciples in a boat and told them to go to the other side of the lake. *He told the disciples to get in a boat.* It's important for us to note that.

After about twelve hours, they were still only about halfway across the lake! Consider what it must have been like to be in a boat with eleven other people for twelve hours during a strong wind that created big waves! The disciples were rowing *against* the wind. What a trial!

Rowing for one hour on a sunny day might pose a challenge for many of us. But sitting in a boat for twelve hours, exhausted and wet in the middle of the night, rowing against the wind, perhaps bailing out water to keep the boat from sinking—well, that's a different story!

The disciples were most likely weary, cold, and apparently fearful for their lives when they saw Jesus approaching them—walking on the water! In fact, at first they thought they were seeing a ghost. But when I read this story I must always remember that *it was Jesus* who told them to get in the boat. Why would He do that? Certainly, being God, He would have known that there was a storm brewing. Certainly He would have known that after twelve hours they would still be far from land, full of despair and discouragement. I must conclude that He was not being malicious in this command to them, but rather that He did this because he had something to teach them about faith.

Eventually Peter recognized Jesus, jumped out of the boat, and walked briefly with Jesus on the water. Peter's plan was soon thwarted when he fell deep into the waves and was about to drown. He uttered his simple and profound plea, "Lord, save me!" Immediately Jesus reached down and pulled him out of the water. Then He calmed the wind.

Make-up Test?

This episode happened immediately after Jesus and the disciples had fed the five thousand. In some ways Jesus probably felt they had

failed that test of faith (John 6:5–7). Therefore, He put them in the
boat for a "make-up test." He thought that there was still some learning to be done. Jesus was *intentionally* investing in His disciples' lives
because He knew what was before them. He knew they would bear
the responsibility of spreading the gospel under tremendous persecu-
tion and eventual death.

Perhaps He especially had Peter in mind. He wanted to grow
his faith, and He knew that trials would make it stronger. Jesus
knew that one day, Peter would be the founder of the church. The
Jewish people would be ushered into a relationship with Jesus, the
fulfillment of their awaited Messiah ("the Anointed One"), and Peter
would be the one used to do this.

Jesus told Peter, "And I tell you that you are Peter, and on this
rock I will build my church, and the gates of Hades will not over-
come it. I will give you the keys of the kingdom of heaven; whatever
you bind on earth will be bound in heaven, and whatever you loose
on earth will be loosed in heaven" (Matt. 16:18–19). Amazingly, He
entrusted this grand movement to Peter, and then began it on the
day of Pentecost through Peter's sermon in Acts 2:14–36. God had
an intentional plan to perfect the disciples' faith by taking them far
outside their comfort zones.

Create Intentional Opportunities

When we find ourselves with our children in places of comfort
and complacency, it's our responsibility to create opportunities to
expose them to situations that will challenge their faith and their
human resources. One way we've done this in our family has been
through mission trips. We decided when our family was young that

we wanted to live in such a way that our children were exposed to many diverse cultures, religious beliefs, sociological demographics, languages, economic situations, and political structures.

Some of that has been through traveling abroad, but some has just been through investing in our community. We live in a cosmopolitan area where there is a diversity of community within a short driving distance from our home. We discovered that our children were forced to depend on God in ways they would have never experienced had they stayed in the safety of our home and our community during their developmental years.

We took our children to senior homes, food kitchens, homeless shelters, and food banks. We also took them field gleaning and to see people living in temporary motel housing. Each of these opportunities gave us a time to be stretched, to be learners about the way others live, to see beauty in places where we least expected it. These experiences enabled us to discuss what Jesus said about such circumstances.

Out of Desperation

When my daughter was only eighteen months old, my husband received a phone call offering him a position teaching at a college in Kenya for three months. My daughter was just a baby, and I wasn't far from that either. I was a very young mom still trying to figure out this whole thing called parenthood. During those months in a little village called Kijabe, I grew in ways that are hard to define.

I grew as a woman, as a mother, as a wife, and as a child of God. I was desperate most days. I cried out to God to help me, support me, strengthen me, and befriend me. I didn't have any of the luxuries that I had at home. I didn't have anything. I didn't have an oven, washer or dryer, hot water, or electricity half the time. I didn't have a phone or a computer or even a friend. I was profoundly lonely, and I was raising a child without the community of my friends or my family in a foreign place.

During those months that would ultimately shape my life as an adult and a parent, God taught me an enormous amount about simplicity and what was most important in the grand scheme of life. By the time I left my tour of duty in Kenya, I felt as though I could conquer anything in parenting with God by my side. Looking back, I see that God was setting up the posture of my heart toward this environment of being out of my comfort zone.

Families on Mission

When we returned from Jenya and had our son just a year later, it never occurred to me to "wait until my children were old enough" to go on mission. I'm so glad God did that for me. I wasn't smart enough to be intentional about it. He just did that for me. But it really made me think, "Well, if I can just sling my daughter on my back in a baby carrier, or if I can put her on my hip in Africa, then why can't I do that *anywhere?*"

So this became a value for us, to raise our children *on mission*— wherever that was. Whether it was taking a neighbor to the doctor, watching someone's children, sacrificially giving to one in need, or choosing to be a friend to the friendless in our community, I wanted our family to grow as people who saw every day as a day to be about God's mission.

As I look at both of my children now, I'm grateful that they are familiar with other languages, that they are comfortable with using different currency, eating a variety of foods, or talking to people of a different color or race. These are just some of the things that take them out of their comfort zones. We never know how God is going to use these abilities in ways that will impact the rest of their lives and the kingdom of God—but I'm excited to see it as their lives continue to unfold.

When our children were little, being out of their comfort zone may simply have meant not having their favorite toy with us while on mission, but now that they're older it seems that it is God who usually keeps the stakes high for them. He is faithful to never let us just "peak" and then say, "Okay, that's enough." We never *arrive*. Not in this life anyway. Paul reminds us of this when he says he is "confident of this, that he who began a good work in you will carry it on to completion until the day of Christ Jesus" (Phil. 1:6). We are a work in progress until we see Jesus face-to-face.

A Generation of Renewed Strength

Of course, there are other situations that take our children out of their comfort zones. Helping them face their fears is a huge part of parenting in this environment. Think about the wide array of fears that children encounter: the fear of meeting new people, swimming, dogs, the dark, sleeping alone, clowns (well, who isn't afraid of that one?), roller coasters, going to a new school or new town, new foods, bugs, that strange aunt, and spiders, just to name a few. You will support your child in growing strong in this area as you *walk through* these fears and trials with them instead of simply *avoiding* them altogether.

Paul also offers encouragement to us as we endure trials and live lives that are outside of where we would normally find comfort. He says, "Therefore we do not lose heart. Though outwardly we are wasting away, yet inwardly we are being renewed day by day. For our light and momentary troubles are achieving for us an eternal glory that far outweighs them all" (2 Cor. 4:16–17).

When we really believe that what God is preparing for us in eternity is far greater than anything we could suffer here on earth, then we are free to live a life of risk and abandonment not bound by fear. A generation empowered with this mind-set will be a generation to be reckoned with—of that I am certain!

8

An Entrusted Kingdom
The Environment of Responsibility

But the trouble with deep belief is that is costs
something. And there is something inside
me, some selfish beast of a subtle thing that
doesn't like the truth at all because it carries
responsibility, and if I actually believe these
things I have to do something about them.

Donald Miller[15]

Burden or Blessing?

If the idea of taking your children out of their comfort zone made
you a bit uncomfortable, maybe you'll like the impact this next
environment has in your home: responsibility. Let's be honest,
though—*responsibility* is a word that can often make us feel burdened. The mere word seems to conjure up feelings about those

things that we *have* to do—not those things that we *get* to do. It can feel like the word *chores* in the environment of service. But to be responsible for someone or something simply makes us account-able. And if I live in an environment where I am not responsible for anything or anyone, I become self-centered, selfish, and myopic in my perspective.

This is why Paul said to the young church in Philippi, "Each of you should look not to your own interests, but also to the interests of others" (Phil. 2:4). He knew that they, like us, would be tempted to live in a way that looked out for "number one" and in doing so would miss out on the adventure to which God was calling them.

In God's kingdom, when He calls us to responsibility, He *entrusts* His plans to us! What an awesome concept: I've been entrusted with accomplishing what God would want me to say or do on His behalf! We truly *get* to be a part of what He is up to, and this is where the fun comes in, for both us and our children.

The Good Samaritan

One day when my daughter was just three-and-a-half years old, my husband was reading his Bible with her at the breakfast table. On a regular basis, he would read Bible stories to her before he left for work—just a few minutes—and then he would elaborate on the story. On this morning he was telling her about the Good Samaritan in Luke 10. After reading through the story and telling her about it, he kissed her and went off to work.

Later that day I picked her up from her preschool play group and asked her if she wanted to get some ice cream. She was thrilled at the prospect. Then we came to a stoplight next to a homeless man standing by the side of the freeway. He was wearing worn clothes, had very few possessions, and held a sign.

My daughter saw him and asked, "What's wrong with that man, and what does his sign say?" I told her his sign said that he was hungry. I explained that he probably didn't have a house, or a job, or even money. This disturbed her. "What do you mean? Where does he sleep? How does he eat?" As I tried my best to explain what happened, she interrupted to announce that we should feed him if he is hungry.

I began to think to myself, "I'm tired.... I want to go home.... I have plans for an ice-cream date with my daughter.... Really, I'm not responsible for this man right now." Because I literally had just five dollars in my wallet, I told my daughter that we could go get him food *or* we could go get ice cream. "What do you want to do?" I asked.

A Lesson in Being Watchful

Well, she definitely wanted to buy him food, so off we went to McDonald's to buy him a Happy Meal. As we drove back by the man on the corner, she rolled down her window and handed him the lunch. As he took the bag from her, he said, "Why thank you, and God bless you." As I drove away, my daughter hollered back out the window, "God bless you!"

I witnessed the joy of giving and taking responsibility for someone in a three-year-old! To see her selflessness and pure motives made me reflect on my own heart. She was already experiencing what God promises us when He says that we are "more blessed to give than to receive" (Acts 20:35). She gave a meal and did not receive ice cream that day. She gave out of a pure heart, when I was not as willing.

That night when my husband came home, she took off running into his arms, shouting, "Daddy, Daddy … you're not going to believe it, but today I was a *Good American.*" Now it's true that she was a good American, but for her, this was an opportunity to live out the story she had heard that morning of the Good Samaritan. I didn't know at the time that he had told her that story at breakfast, but at the age of three, already God's Spirit was using her in helping someone who was in need.

My husband had told her that morning, "Now that you've heard this story I want you to look all through the day—be *watchful,* look for somebody who needs your help. Be aware. Have your eyes wide open. Look, because God's going to have someone in your path that you're going to be able to help, and He wants you to help take responsibility for him or her." Well, in doing this, he piqued her curiosity. He piqued her thoughts, and all day long she was looking. So much so that when she saw this man who needed a lunch, it was compelling for her, and she experienced faith in action.

So as my children left for school in the years that followed that day, I would often tell them things to look for. I would say that somebody might need a kind word, and I'd encourage each of them to look for that person. Or I might tell them how generous they were, and that God wanted to use their generosity. I would say, "Be watchful for someone today. Look for a way to encourage someone, or look for a way to be honest when other people are being dishonest."

Then later that day at dinner, I would ask them if they were able to find a way to do the things we discussed. We realized that these opportunities are in our life every day—but sometimes we're just not looking for them. When we are awakened to what God is doing all around us, taking responsibility becomes being a part of something so much bigger than ourselves.

An All-Encompassing Call

Ultimately, the concept of creating an environment of responsibility in our homes is a charge from God that encompasses a variety of areas. First, it captures the ability to take ownership before God for one's life, gifts, and resources. Second, it challenges us to take responsibility for those in our family and our spiritual family in Christ, for their well-being. Lastly, it calls us to seek out in love those who are hurting, poor, and spiritually lost, recognizing our responsibility to those who don't yet know Jesus and His forgiveness.

The early church described in the book of Acts took these three things seriously. As they were awakened to their new life in Christ through the Holy Spirit, they lived radically different lives. With great sacrifice, they generously gave of their time, talents, money, homes, and meals to anyone who was part of their new family in God. In addition, these same people sought to take care of the poor, the outcast, the lost, and the homeless in their towns. They lived what they believed, and it was compelling to those who were watching. In this environment where each person took responsibility for himself and for those around him, the church grew like wildfire! It was unstoppable.

The Law of Sowing and Reaping

One foundational aspect of responsibility is sowing and reaping. Many of us don't live in an agrarian culture where children are familiar with farming techniques. But for those who do, farming is one of the most powerful means to help children understand the law of sowing and reaping. In sowing and reaping, what you plant is what you get.

Farmers learn how much the environment has to do with what they plant. And what they plant in the ground and what comes up out of it correspond to each other. You don't plant corn seeds and get a peach tree. What you plant is what you get. Paul made this point clear to the Galatians:

> Do not be deceived: God cannot be mocked. A man reaps what he sows. The one who sows to please his sinful nature, from that nature will reap destruction; the one who sows to please the Spirit, from the Spirit will reap eternal life. Let us not become weary in doing good, for at the proper time we will reap a harvest if we do not give up. Therefore, *as we have opportunity, let us do good to all people*, especially to those who belong to the family of believers. (6:7–10)

When my children were little, I wanted them to have this experiential understanding of sowing and reaping, so we planted a garden. I knew that in school they had put a lima bean in a cup with a wet cotton ball. They learned that it would sprout. But this was different. I actually wanted them to garden, to have to take care of something. So we shopped for seeds—all kinds of them. Tomato seeds, green pepper seeds, corn seeds, watermelon seeds, and a variety of flower seeds filled the patch of dirt next to our house.

Each of my children planted the seeds and then labeled them so that they would remember what they had *sown*. They were watchful to see if that was the same thing that they would *reap*. Of course, they had to weed the garden, prune it, water it, care for it, and then wait for the fruit or flower to blossom. When it did, we celebrated!

Teachable Moments

Now why is this so important? If you invest in a garden, you will be able to draw from this analogy for the rest of your children's lives. For one, they will always relate to Jesus' metaphors about farming, pruning, the soil, the seeds, and the weeds. Think of how many stories in Scripture have to do with this concept!

It also gives them responsibility over something. If they have responsibility over a garden, it helps them understand that their actions have an effect on what happens. If they choose not to give it water, it will die. If they choose not to pull out the weeds, it won't bear as much fruit. If they choose to trample over it when they're playing soccer, they won't have the fruit at all. Yet when they faithfully invest, the reward will come.

Responsibility as an environment extends beyond our home life. There are many things for which we need to instill this sense of responsibility in our children. We need to create opportunities where our children can take ownership of not only their family members, but also others, their community, their school, their money, their time, and their talents. If you think about all the things we are responsible for in order to call ourselves adults they're abundant. Responsibility is foundational to life. How will our children invest in their schoolwork, give their all for the team on the playing field, stick by a friend during a trying time, and eventually apply this to their marriage relationship and family members? Nurturing an environment of responsibility now has a lifetime of dividends.

Responsibility for My Life and My World

Before I can be responsible for anyone else, I must take responsibility for *me*. This is not a selfish act, but a necessary one. My friend Roger Tirabassi illustrated this point well when he said that the airline companies understand this concept when they instruct passengers, "In the event of an emergency, if you are traveling with a child, *first* put on your own oxygen mask *before* putting on the mask of your child." By taking responsibility for myself, I am in a better position to offer myself to others.

Our role as parents is to teach our children to be responsible for their bodies and their lives. Consider the abundance of areas that we seek to cover before our children leave home. We need to teach them how to maintain personal hygiene, clean their room and make their bed, practice table manners and eating habits, get healthy exercise, calculate math problems, write a good sentence, know Jesus and God's Word, do the laundry, make a meal, look at someone in the eye when they are speaking, shake a hand, sit quietly, speak up, be punctual, manage money, drive a car, interact with the opposite sex, interact with extended family, say "please" and "thank you"—and mean it … and the list goes on.

I believe that one of the reasons God put children in the home where parents are the primary teachers of these things is because He knows that as children grow in an environment where they are responsible for the above list (and more), the Spirit works within them to cultivate a harvest of righteousness. Responsibility lays a foundation that underlies every other aspect of our lives, and yet parents so often neglect it because we are too busy, weary, or feel ill equipped to get the desired results. Whatever the barriers, spiritual parents must take this task seriously. The Spirit uses this character quality in an individual as a means for spiritual transformation.

Because there are so many categories within taking responsibility for self and others, and because there are many parenting books that focus on such things, I will address just one of the issues of personal responsibility that I feel has far-extending impact. This is the issue of money management.

Managing Money

Managing money is a biblical principle—yet we live in a society that says we all *deserve* to have what we want, when we want it. Instant gratification is lord of our universe. Children adopt this posture quickly in life, and very often money is the source of fulfilling their desires. The debt of our nation, and each person in it, is staggering. As we pursue a mentality of "buy now and pay later," we rob ourselves and our children of the opportunity to take responsibility. The responsible thing to say is, "If I don't have the money, then I can't have the item/experience," but instead entitlement creeps in and this form of pride wages war against responsibility.

Because my husband and I were aware of this subtle seduction, and because I myself had been so swept away in it during my college years, we decided that we would attempt to help our children manage money from an early age. When our children were in their elementary years, we began to give them a certain amount of money to manage throughout the month.

In some instances this may have been more money than most of their friends were receiving for an "allowance," but with it *they* had to manage it according to the many needs and desires that would arise. This included gifts for the myriad birthday parties they were invited to, times they wanted to stop for fast food on a whim, or toys they wanted to buy. Within this model, they could take responsibility to look at their money and then choose to manage it accordingly. As my children got older, we increased their budget in order for them to purchase almost everything needed, except for what was provided in our home.

To Tithe or Not to Tithe?

One of the teachings about money in the Old Testament is the concept of tithing. Now the tithe (or *tenth*) was a part of the way the Hebrew people lived. Whether it was your flocks, your monetary earnings, even your herbs—whatever it was—one-tenth of it was brought into the storehouse and used for several things. These offerings took care of the poor, the needy, and the widows in their community. In addition, the tithe took care of the priests and the people who were part of the tribe of Levi. It was how this community was instructed to take responsibility for one another. It was non-negotiable. *Everybody* gave 10 percent.

As we translate this concept into today's society, there are a couple of things that we want to make note of in regard to our children. The first is that many times churches merely teach tithing without the larger context of *why*. When I was a child, I was taught that I should do this, that I should give 10 percent of my money to God, because it was right. Certainly we could argue this perspective, but there is a much bigger issue here. By just tithing out of duty, I can simply write my check and cross it off of my to-do list. It is tempting to feel righteous because I do, and that becomes a behaviorist way of approaching my spirituality.

Instead, let's remember some of the things that Jesus said about money or giving in the New Testament: Give generously. Give cheerfully. So often, people who look at the New Testament standards and consider tithing think that Jesus "let us off the hook" because we are now under grace. But in actuality, the stakes got much higher! Instead of God saying, "I require of you 10 percent," He now says, "I want you to give generously."

Generously and Cheerfully with Abandonment

What is enormously powerful about this statement is that we have to be in *relationship* with Him to figure out what *generous* is. This was a huge "Aha" for me. Maybe generous for someone is 30 percent, or maybe it's 50 percent. I know of an individual who lives off only 40 percent of his income and is giving generously of the remaining 60 percent. Sixty percent!

It also means that we must give it *cheerfully*. Note that Jesus does not say to give dutifully or piously. If we understand that all of what we have belongs to God, He doesn't just get 10 percent. My pastor, Mike Erre, says, "Instead of asking the question, 'How much of my money does God get?' I need to ask the question, 'How much of God's money am I going to keep?'" This is a revolutionary way of thinking, and it is imperative that we pass this on to our children.

I do think it's good to train children to set aside a portion of their money to give generously, and if you want to make that portion 10 percent, then great. Sometimes it's easy for them to figure out that if they have ten dollars, then one dollar goes here. But children are generous, and I bet if you challenge your children to be aware of what the needs are and how they can be generous, and if you expose them to these things, there will be times when they give the whole ten dollars.

Consider the widow in the Bible who gave out of her poverty (Luke 21:4). The original Greek word for this impoverishment means to be destitute or desperate. What does it mean for me to give out of my desperation? In this story, wealthy people were dumping boatloads of money into the collection box at the temple, but then a poor widow came and gave all she had—she gave out of true destitution. She gave 100 percent! What was it about that woman that was so beautiful to Jesus? Was it that she was giving cheerfully? She wasn't calculating, "Okay, what's 10 percent of two mites?" No, she just gave with abandonment.

Children can have this posture and grow in it within the environment of responsibility. What would our world look like if a new generation felt responsible for the world they lived in and gave generously, sacrificially, and with abandonment? I want my children to live in a world like that!

Responsibility to Our Community

One night my children and I were taking a walk. It was when our neighborhood was relatively new, and they were still building homes and other structures. There was a church that was being built right in the middle of our neighborhood. As we walked by, we saw the signs that said that they were getting ready to do a grand opening in just a few days. For weeks prior, we had been walking by it every night and watching how it was progressing—first the structure, then the paint, and finally the landscaping.

Just days before our walk, the church had covered the campus with beautiful grass sod. However, on this particular night when we walked by, we realized that somebody had run donuts on the grass with their car and torn up a large portion of the sod. It looked horrible. We stopped and discussed it, and we were sad knowing that Sunday was coming and the church had worked so hard for their big launch.

As we walked by, I said to my children, "Do you realize how sad these people will be when they come to church on Sunday morning and their grass is all torn up and ruined—after all that they've sacrificed?" I went on, "Whose responsibility is that?" They replied, "Well, the people who did it, of course." And I said, "That's true— and do you think that the people who did that are going to come back and fix it?" They said, "No." I went on to ask them who else's responsibility it might be to fix it. They mentioned the people at the church, the gardener, even the pastor.

I shared that I didn't know who would be responsible in the church, but that there was a good possibility that they might not even get here until Sunday—and it would be too late. "So," I asked again, "whose responsibility is it?" They were starting to say to themselves, "Oh no, she's going to say *us,* isn't she?!" They looked at me sheepishly and responded in unison, "We are"—half as a statement, and half as a question. I wanted to probe further, "Okay, *why* are we responsible?" As we explored this question, each of us began to see that grassy field and that church in a new way.

We were responsible for that situation because we were fellow believers with the people in that church. They were our brothers and sisters in Christ, even though we had not met them yet. We were responsible because we lived in that neighborhood. Because of this, the grass needed to be fixed, and it needed to be fixed before Sunday.

When we give our children tangible faith opportunities to put what we're teaching them into action, then we create environments for God's Spirit to work in their hearts and lives. This is why it's crucial to look for opportunities. We must have our eyes wide open, be attentive to God's Spirit, and be prayerful, asking God to teach us to parent in these spiritually forming ways.

A Change of Heart Needed

If I'm honest, I know how often I fall short of seizing these teachable moments. These situations are often hard to navigate because I'm not necessarily the person I want my children to be. This can be a struggle, because I desperately want to teach my children to be sacrificial and other-centered, to have eyes to see the needs around them, and then to take responsibility for what God is asking them to do. So this is why so much of being a spiritual parent is about the work that God wants to do in each of us—first.

As our Father, God is creating learning environments for us as well! But when I blow it—when I don't model responsibility—I then go back and *redeem* it. I tell my kids, "You know what? I should've taken responsibility for this or that, but I didn't. I missed out on that blessing. I know God is going to do it. God will accomplish what He wants to, but I could've been part of His Big Story in this way—and I blew it this time. So I'm going to look for another opportunity. Next time I can do that differently."

When I'm tired, I ask God for strength. I can even stop and pray, in front of my children, so that they understand that I choose to be responsible for myself and others out of God's strength and not my own. I want to be an accurate role model—there's no use in my being a supermom in their eyes.

To be a spiritual parent means that I will live an authentic life before my children and allow them to be eyewitnesses to my own faith journey. All of us at one time or another have experienced this pull toward being selfish. But since responsibility is something God is asking of us, we can pray and ask Him to change our hearts.

This kind of authentic life, in which we openly take responsibility for our mistakes, makes us far more effective when our children mess up and we have to visit the next environment: course correction.

9

Discipline That Heals

The Environment of Course Correction

That's how God chose to reveal to us the
divine love, bring us back into an embrace
of compassion, and convince us that anger
has been melted away in endless mercy.

Henri Nouwen[16]

Biblical Discipline

In the realm of spiritual parenting, discipline elicits more questions than any other subject. The environment of course correction describes biblical discipline. However, I chose the words *course correction,* because I love the metaphorical picture of what it means to correct one's course.

As parents, the discipline of our children is probably one of the most time- and energy-intensive aspects of our daily lives. How ought we to discipline our children, and how does that discipline reflect who God is? The answers to these questions make the role of parenting something we can't take lightly!

In chapters 3–5 we talked about setting a strong foundation for identity in Christ in the big picture narrative and in the faith family that God has graciously invited each of us to be a part of. Next, we discussed how that foundation could be used for a greater pursuit than our own self-interest. The environments of service, out of the comfort zone, and responsibility cultivate hearts that are outwardly focused. Yet in all of these endeavors, our children will fall short and need course correction.

From Pain to Healing

Often our desperation can drive us to seek any book, person, or strategy that might bring clarity on how to conquer this grand assignment. This task of biblical discipline can be exhausting and bring even the most dedicated of parents to their knees—which, ironically, is the first place that a spiritual parent needs to begin. Instead of relying on our own wisdom and strength or giving up altogether, we must first come to Jesus and ask Him, "How would You like me to bring correction to this child You have given me?" In this act of surrender, we are ready to understand what God desires for us most in course correction.

The author of Hebrews explains how course correction works:

> No discipline seems pleasant at the time, but
> painful. Later on, however, it produces a harvest
> of righteousness and peace for those who have
> been trained by it.

Therefore, strengthen your feeble arms and weak
knees. "Make level paths for your feet," so that
the lame may not be disabled, but rather healed.
(12:11–13)

As we seek God in this passage for His design of discipline, it's
imperative that we don't stop at verse 11. While we might agree that
"no discipline seems pleasant at the time, but painful," if we simply stop there we might be led to believe that discipline is merely a
painful and negative experience. That kind of discipline deserves a
different name: *punishment*. Where punishment prevails, we almost
always find several other things: hiding, blame, guilt, and shame. Yet
the goal of biblical discipline is altogether different—it is far more
redemptive!

The Problem with Punishment

If only pain and punishment follow my wrong actions, then it doesn't
take me long to create a backup plan. Some children (and adults)
decide that doing the deed is not worth the consequence, and they
may stop the sin or action from a place of willpower. They try harder
to not sin or mess up, and life becomes a journey of what Dallas
Willard calls "sin management." The problem with this approach is
that the root issue remains unchanged in the person. It's not given
the opportunity to come into the light and receive restoration. As
children grow into adults, they become more and more aware of
their depravity, and sin management can become a full-time job!
Because the root is merely managed and never dealt with, shame and
guilt prevail—and these things make us want to hide from God.

Remember Adam and Eve? When they sinned and their eyes were opened to good and evil, they recognized their failure. Yet, fearing God—and how He might "punish" them—they quickly began to blame, hide, and experience guilt and shame. God came to them and called them out of hiding to deal with their sin openly and honestly.

Now of course there were consequences for their actions, but God also promised that He would set up a corrective course—not only for Adam and Eve, but for all of humanity. He promised that a Redeemer would come someday, and this redeemer would give people a chance for victory and restoration. Adam and Eve, like us, needed something so much bigger than a punishment. They needed a solution that didn't simply manage the situation but rather corrected it for good.

In our home we decided that we would not use the word *punishment* for several reasons. If you look at the passage from Hebrews 12, there's nothing in it about punishment. Biblically, punishment is receiving God's wrath. Now there are times when I'm sure you are like me, and you want nothing more than for your child to receive God's wrath! But in Christ, we don't suffer God's wrath. Hallelujah!

Therefore, we want to carefully model for our children what it means to actually walk in *the path of the Divine*. We want to bring them into what is true and real by exposing them to God and His plan for their lives. When they fail—and they will—we want to bring to them course correction so that they understand their standing with a holy God.

Healing from Sin

So what is the goal of course correction? If punishment's goal is God's wrath, then according to the verses in Hebrews, what is the goal of course correction or biblical discipline? It is found in the last word of verse 13: *healing*. The end goal for us as parents is to conduct God's discipline in our children's lives in such a way that they experience healing from their sin. Did you catch that? Read it again: *The end goal for us as parents is to conduct God's discipline in our children's lives in such a way that they experience healing from their sin.*

If we can embrace this reality in our homes, then our children, through Christ, will ultimately experience spiritual healing. Few people will acknowledge feeling just as loved in their sin as they do in their success. But this is a biblical concept for those who are in Christ. There is nothing that can separate us from God's love (Rom. 8:38–39). Our standing with God is not shaken when we need correction; rather our heart needs healing. What better time to receive love than when you are wounded? What would it look like for our children to experience such grace?

Spiritual Formation versus Behavior Modification

I am often struck—when I am at a grocery store, a bank, a park—by the amount of wrath-of-God discipline that I witness. I remember when, as a young mom who felt powerless, I used these techniques myself. Wrath-of-God discipline has some common phrases (see if you can relate): "If you don't stop pulling on your sister's hair, you will regret it"—or, "Just wait until your father gets home, and then you're going to be in really big trouble." Or maybe you have been told or have heard someone say this: "I'll spank you so hard that you won't be able to sit for a week," or, "Stop crying, or I'll really give you something to cry about!" We could all come up with a few classic phrases that our parents said to us, right? But all of them basically carry the connotation that "you'll be so sad, sorry, pained, or wounded that you'll never want to do 'this' again."

Unfortunately, this is not the purpose of course correction. This purpose is not merely to have my child incur such a negative experience that he or she doesn't want to do "it" again. Ultimately, the purpose of discipline is to create an environment where the root problem is exposed and healed so that it no longer causes the negative behavior. This is true spiritual formation, but so often we settle for behavior modification!

Even when our children are little, the reason why they do the things they do—such as being selfish or defiant, or having a bad attitude—is that there's a root problem, the problem of sin. Our goal in course correction is to align their hearts with a path of healing that only God can bring. When we do this, we allow our children to be honest about their sin, not to hide it or manage it in their flesh, and by doing so we help them begin to understand *why* they need a Savior. This is fundamental to their faith. So as we look at Hebrews 12, keep in mind that our goal in biblical discipline is spiritual transformation. It's always *this kind* of healing, whether they are one year old or eighteen years old.

At the Heart of the Matter

We often need to ask our child the kinds of questions that get to the heart of the matter in order to bring healing. If our questions hover at the ground level of the actual behavior, we erroneously focus on the outcome rather than on the source. It's tempting to do this in our busy schedules, to settle for a discipline model that demands, "Just stop that ugly behavior … NOW!"

However, spiritual parenting digs deeper to penetrate the heart and give the child a glimpse of his soul and his motivation toward sin. This is a tool parents can give their children so that when they're older and Mom and Dad aren't around, they can say with conviction, "Search me and know me, God. Search my heart, and let me know if there's any wicked way within me" (see Psalm 139:23–24).

When my son, Brendon, was fifteen he loved to skateboard. He spent hours every afternoon skating through parks, down stairs, and finding the perfect spot for the perfect trick. I often played chauffeur for him and his friends as they scouted out these choice areas for thrill and risk. As I drove them from site to site, I heard their conversations and the words they used to describe others or an event—and not all of them were edifying. Far from it.

Occasionally, if one boy felt another had crossed the line, he'd say, "Hey, watch what you say," and the offender would apologize. One night, I had dropped off all the boys, and my son and I went to dinner together. I was thrilled to have him all to myself to share life over a meal.

Now in the world of teenage boys, one-word grunts usually suffice for communication. "Are you hungry?" [Grunt] "Do you have homework?" [Grunt] "Did you have fun?" [Grunt] It's a gripping exchange of ideas! So as we sat down to eat, my son grunted. But it was good because he was grunting *with me*, and I wanted him to know I was interested in his life.

And then he actually crafted an entire sentence—in the form of a question, no less. He said, "Hey Mom, does it bother you when my friends are swearing? … Well, would it bother you if *I* used those bad words?" Wow! I knew this was a moment I didn't want to blow. I prayed a quick prayer and thought of my options.

Option one was to say, "Of course it would bother me to have you cuss or swear! Don't you know who I am? You wouldn't want to embarrass me at the church, would you? Besides—it's just horrible, and you shouldn't do it. Case closed!" Option two, however, raced through my mind like a subtle wind and seemed to get at the heart of the matter.

I said, "Brendon, what I am most concerned about is your heart. This is what God is most concerned about too. So I don't want you to use bad language simply because everyone else is doing it and you want to fit in, but I also don't want you to not swear only because your father and I say not to. You're old enough to determine what is in your heart and then to speak words that are congruent with who you are." I waited, but there was no grunt. He nodded and then began to share about his day, his thoughts, his life.

We sat in that café for over an hour just *talking*—sharing about decision making in the most delicate of teenage topics. A waitress overhearing our conversation walked by at one point and just mouthed the words "Oh my gosh!" to me. She was amazed at the level at which we were sharing—and quite frankly so was I! It is one of my most treasured moments with my son, because I let God use my words to penetrate the heart and not just the behavior. He felt safe in that moment to desire healing.

Step One: It Must Be Painful

Hebrews 12 outlines a three-step process for course correction. In verse 11, it says, "No discipline seems pleasant at the time, but painful." The first step is *pain*. Now you might say, "Well, pain actually sounds the same as God's wrath—that doesn't sound like healing." But in reality, true healing starts with pain. So the first step to biblical discipline or course correction is to determine pain.

We need God to figure this part out, because each child is wired differently, and pain for one child is different from pain for another child. But, what often happens in our homes is that we adopt a *parenting model*, and we say that in our home we don't spank, or in our home we only spank, or in our home we do time-outs, and so on. But, what I'd encourage you to do is to think back to Proverbs 22:6, which urges us to "train a child *in the way he should go*." As you take into account the personality and inner makeup of your child and how she responds to you and to circumstances, then you can identify what pain is for her. You can adopt a *child-specific* discipline model.

For instance, when my daughter was little, if I gave her a swat on the behind, she would turn around to me (now remember, this is the one who told me I was only third in charge) and say, "Mommy, it doesn't hurt." Maybe you have this kind of a child! I would have literally had to wound her before she would ever have gotten to the place of "pain," because her will was stronger than the physical pain. So in essence, getting physical was counterproductive.

My son, on the other hand, was different. If I even just showed him a wooden spoon or told him he would get a spanking, that was corrective for him. A stern look and voice were his pain most of the time when he was young. On the other hand, my daughter hated to go in time-outs, because that meant she was away from all of the action. If I sent my son to his room for time-outs, he would think, "Cool, alone time ... this is great." So that was not *pain* for him, but it was for my daughter. Of course as they grew older, we were always reassessing what was painful. As our children gained more and more freedoms, we also had more avenues to determine a particular path of pain designed especially for them!

I had to determine that instead of having a parenting style, I needed to have a child-specific style. I needed to tailor a program for each of my children with God's help in order to accomplish what was best for the way they were created. Think about it: This is the way God deals with us. God doesn't just sit up in heaven and say, "All of you millions and billions of people: This is the predetermined path if you disobey," as if we are all like cattle walking through life.

Instead He customizes specific life experiences, specific trials, and very loving environments for us as individuals. How does He do that? Well, I'm in awe of it. I'm grateful that He takes that much care and love to tailor a path for *me*, because He cares about *my* healing. But as wonderful as this sounds, we can't get there without pain—we have to experience the pain.

Step Two: Build Them Up in Love

If the first stage of biblical course correction is pain, but we know that the harvest comes when we move past mere punishment, then we must read on to see what redemptive pieces are available in the Hebrews 12 passage. The second stage comes from verse 12: "Strengthen your feeble arms and weak knees." Think about this for a minute. This is a word picture of arms and knees that have broken down. The parts of the body that allow us to move forward productively have gone limp.

That first step of pain has broken down the child's will, bringing them to a place of submission. This step is necessary, but it's
destructive if the child stays in a broken state. Therefore, step two is
strengthening what you broke down. So in course correction, immediately after we bring the pain we also bring restitution to that child
in love, in reassurance, and in encouragement. It's important to note
that the one who brings the pain must also be the one who brings the
love and encouragement.

Consider what this might look like. After you have disciplined
your child with the appropriate measure of pain, whatever the pain
is, he immediately needs a moment of eye-to-eye contact with you. I
used to get down on my knees or get level with my children so they
knew I was attentive. I placed them on my lap when they were little,
or now that my son is a teenager I sit with him, and I make sure he
knows I want to have a connection. This takes effort and practice.
We need to learn the art of speaking *to* our children and not *at* them.
This includes having a dialogue, not just a monologue where we
dominate the conversation.

I said, "I love you," because after failing or sinning, children
need to hear these words. I continued, "I know you're probably not
really happy with me right now, but the reason I'm disciplining you
is because I love you." And even if they didn't buy it or rolled their
eyes (which they sometimes did), they needed to hear it from me.

Next they needed affection. I hugged my children, even if they
didn't hug back in the moment. I touched their shoulder or their
leg—something physical to tell them I wasn't shunning them.

Finally, I offered words of encouragement. I said something about
them that I appreciated, such as a humble spirit or a willingness to

listen. I told them I knew that next time they were going to be able to make this decision better with God's help.

This encouragement gives them hope, and without it the Enemy will lie to our children and convince them that *they can never change*. By giving them hope, we're telling them we believe in them. So often in a punishment model, we say things like, "You're *always* doing this," or, "I'm so fed up that you *keep* making these bad choices," or, "You'll *never* change."

There are other things we sometimes say in anger that discourage children and keep them from being strengthened. For example, we can burden them with more responsibility for the act than what the natural consequences were. We do this with words like, "Do you realize how much stress this is putting on your father and me?" or, "We are fighting all the time because you can't seem to behave," or, "Don't you understand how financially debilitating this is to us?" or, "If I get one more phone call from your teacher, I won't be able to show my face in public." All of these things say in sublime yet powerful ways that we don't believe in them and that they can't change. But encouragement says, "I believe in you. I believe you can do this differently."

Step Three: Make a Straight and Level Path

The third step in God's plan for course correction is stated in Hebrews 12:13: "'Make level paths for your feet,' so that the lame may not be disabled, but rather healed." Making a level path for our children's feet is simply plotting out the new course for them. Here we teach them what it means to change and acknowledge that they will need God's help to do this. Making a level path is telling them you have an idea of how they can navigate differently should the experience arise again, and then walking through those steps. This is where God can use our wisdom gained from having lived and made our own mistakes. We share ourselves with our children candidly.

Let's use an example here: A friend of mine was having difficulty getting her five-year-old son to obey. When she called him in from playing or asked him to clean his room, she had to ask him ten times before he reluctantly obeyed. As parents, we deal with similar situations a lot. My friend wanted to use biblical course correction, because she kept finding herself yelling in exasperation by the tenth time. So she decided that the "pain" would be to take away his TV privileges, his play date, and a favorite toy. She took the time to think through what would be extremely painful (but not harmful) for her unique child.

Then it was time to strengthen him—to build him up in love. So she sat down with him and said, "I know it's a bummer to be cooped up. The weather's so nice, and I know you probably want to be with your friends or playing with your toys. And I know you're unhappy." She acknowledged where he was at, and in doing so she gave him language for his feelings.

She went on, "But I love you, and I'm not doing this to hurt you. I'm doing this because I love you, and I want you to be able to say, 'Yes, Mommy' on the first time. And I want you to have an obedient heart." She explained this while hugged him, then said, "I believe God will help you to do this next time. Let's ask Him by praying. Next time when I ask you to do something, I want you to say, 'Yes, Mommy' the very first time, and then we're going to celebrate. I know you can do that. So let's practice doing it." Then she gave him an opportunity to practice saying it, and they celebrated together. When she did this, she made a straight path for him.

So these are the three things: We break them down in pain, we build them up in love, and then we show them a straight path. We need to be firm in this, because children have a way of making us weary. They wear us down. We're tired. They team up on us! It's horrible. But that's why it's critical to begin this process by saying, "I will parent the way God is asking me to parent because I believe that there will be a harvest."

The Harvest

The final piece of this discipline journey is that, later on, this corrective path produces *a harvest of righteousness and peace.* This is part of the beautiful outcome. If I want anything for my children, it's righteousness and peace! What could be better? Imagine yourself lying in bed at night and saying, "My child walks a righteous life before God, and he is at peace." What more would you want?

When we live in a world where people are in tremendous turmoil (we've never had more people medicating themselves for all sorts of anxieties) and where righteousness is the oddity instead of the norm, even among Christ-followers, what better thing could we desire than to create an environment where God can work in our children's lives on this path of course correction?

Keep in mind that the fruit is righteousness and peace for those *who have been trained by it.* So this is not a onetime event—and that's what is so tiring about being a parent. One day we might feel we were enormously victorious, and then the very next day it just all comes unraveled. But as spiritual parents, we can't give up! I counsel parents all the time who've totally given up. Their children are running amuck. There's absolutely no discipline in the home. There's no path being set out for them. And the result is that children are insecure and lack righteousness and peace. You can look at children and tell if they're being trained by course correction or not. You can tell if their parents have given up.

So don't give up. It's a *training process*. Any sport you train in takes time, effort, and energy—you do it again and again and again. Eventually, you build that muscle. No matter where you are in the path of success in doing this, I want to congratulate you if you have not given up! That alone is commendable. It is critical that you stay firm and focused on the goal—your children's future peace and righteousness hang in the balance.

This is such a crucial environment, because it breeds two vital things: righteousness and peace. These set a foundation for our children to hear God's voice, to know Him, and to obey Him. But sustaining this environment takes a tremendous amount of love. Can we do this in our own strength? No. We need to be relying on God's Spirit to teach us how to parent. I cannot tell you the amount of times I've cried out to God, "Teach me how to parent this daughter; teach me how to parent this son." And He has been faithful to me every time!

A Story of Course Correction

My daughter loves to surf. When she was sixteen she went to the surf shop one day to check out selling her board on consignment in order to upgrade to a better one. One of the salesmen started talking to her about a custom-made surfboard. He detailed the intricate options.

Her excitement built. He said, "I can do it myself, and I'll do it for you at cost—so just tell me, how would you dream it?" Never once did he mention the price, and apparently she didn't ask. Since she had a surfboard, he put it on consignment to use toward the cost, mentioning that the balance should be very little.

In the weeks that passed, this custom board was being made, and the bill was getting higher and higher. She didn't bring her father or me into this conversation. Then one day while she and I were getting a manicure, and I noticed a look of terror on her face when the phone rang. Her answer was an awkward interchange, and then she hung up. I asked, "Who was that?" With that, she burst into tears.

She told me how the salesman at the surf shop had been badgering her daily because she owed him a lot of money for a surfboard that she had ordered. I asked, "What do you mean you ordered a surfboard?" She told me the whole story. "How much do you owe him?" I asked. She looked at the ground and said, "Well, I, uh, I owe him a thousand dollars." What! One thousand dollars? How did this happen? She had a job working ten hours a week making minimum wage. I did the math, thinking how many *years* it would take for us to arrive at "healing."

I prayed in that moment that God would direct my words, and thankfully we had a great conversation. It was a poignant reminder of what happens when we fail. We really have two options, both as children to our parents and also with God: We can either run to our father or mother and confess everything, or we can hide. And how we respond to our children has a direct impact on their understanding of whether they can run to us because they know we will help them receive healing, or whether they will hide out of shame and guilt.

Shock and Appall

One of the reasons our children hide is because of what I call "shocked-and-appalled syndrome." When our children say or do something, and we say, "You *WHAT?!!*"—that's shocked and appalled. Shocked-and-appalled syndrome makes children internalize feelings that what they did must be shameful. They process that what they did is so shocking that they must just be hideously sinful. This can breed in children a tendency to hide.

Children soon learn that any sin might be met with disapproval, so they hide it. The result is that the child doesn't deal with the sin or heal it, but merely "stuffs" it. And what is dangerous is that we have a tendency to carry this habit into our relationship with God. That's why this environment is so important. Because when we as parents model to our children a response to sin, their minds transfer that model to what God must be thinking or feeling. No matter what our children do or say, ultimately we want them to run to us—*straight to us*—so that we can help them and bring them to restoration.

So my daughter had been hiding—and I know that I'd had my fair share of shocked-and-appalled moments while I was raising her. Sadly, they were over insignificant things. But she had been hiding this until it finally came out that day. I wanted to do the shocked-and-appalled response, but instead I had learned to take a moment—because spiritual parenting reminds us to take a moment to pray. So I responded by commenting that, indeed, it was a lot of money, and I asked her what her plan was to pay for it. I quickly realized that there was no plan as she sat there sobbing. So we went to work on a plan, together.

Natural Consequences

Sometimes in course correction, pain is obvious. It's the natural consequence. I love it when pain is the natural consequence, because I don't have to think of some clever thing that seems totally detached. In this case, the natural pain was that after her father and I had paid for the board, she would not be able to surf on it until we were paid back. The second natural pain was that she had to pay us back. So first she needed another job, and between the two jobs I would receive three-fourths of all of her income. That's natural pain. So week after week she was being trained by natural pain.

As we moved from *pain*, we also sat down with her to tell her how much we loved her—*to build her up in love*. We told her that we understood how what she did could have happened and that we were going to support her through this. We encouraged her. Then we marked out the days on the calendar until we knew her debt would be paid.

Next, we wanted to give her a *straight path*. We told her that next time when she was tempted to buy something, she should simply ask how much it cost. Further, we instructed her to invite her father and me into the conversation. We affirmed that everybody makes mistakes and that this was a great opportunity to learn.

Ultimately, God was using this situation for healing in her life. Prior to this event, my daughter wasn't a good manager of her money—at all. Yet now, as she is off at college I see her system of living out of cash envelopes and how she chooses to live below her means in order to be generous with others! I am so proud of her, and I am so thankful to God. He brought healing to her life in an area that will affect many important decisions in the years to come.

Time to Celebrate

One day, she finally made her last payment to us, and that's when the celebration broke out. We got out the surfboard. We oohed and ahhed, and she surfed on it for the first time. It was hers—she had earned it. It was her senior year at that point, and so we decided to have her senior photos taken with her board! We hoped that she would forever look at this picture and remember her healing process.

This surfboard has become an icon for financial healing in my daughter's life. It was even designed with a peace symbol on it, which ironically is exactly what God promises will belong to those who have been healed. When I look at it, I think, "God, You are so good," because I'm aware of how many of us struggle with finances and spending habits as adults. When I look back, it could have been so much different. If we had responded with the wrath-of-God kind of punishment, telling her she would never have that board and shaming her, then we might not have ever gotten to the root of the problem. And the root of the problem was that her eyes were bigger than her financial means and she wanted instant gratification.

Today as you listen to God about the issues deep in your children's hearts, make yourself available to the wisdom in Hebrews 12:11–13. Seek a child-specific pain, build your child up in love and affirmation, and then set forth a straight path for him to walk in. When you do these things, watch for the fruit of righteousness and peace. It doesn't happen overnight, but as you train your children in this environment, God will be faithful to bring healing to their souls.

Course correction is a loving, respectful—and productive—way of dealing with our children's misdeeds. Some parents forget that the manner in which we course correct is as important as getting our children to behave well. To usher in love and respect when children are misbehaving actually represents our heavenly Father's best intentions. Love and respect are so important that they are an environment we need to provide for our children no matter what their behavior or the circumstance.

10

Down at Eye Level

The Environment of Love and Respect

I want to live in such a way that I don't lose
sight of what's important or lose a sense of
the sacredness of others. I want to live in a
way so that I can see windows of the soul.

Ken Gire[17]

Nothing Else Matters

Love and respect. These words represent two of our greatest desires. Is there anything more innate to who we are as human beings? I doubt it.

When we stand back and take a good long look at our job as parents, we can sum it up by saying our role is to love our children. To love them in the way that Christ would love them if He were mom, if He were dad. That's a tall order! In 1 Corinthians 13, Paul gets to the heart of the matter when he describes a multitude of glorious things that we can accomplish in life, yet warns that if we don't do them in love they amount to nothing … and in some cases they're even worse than nothing—they're damaging.

Love is primary, and respect is also of enormous importance because it's critical to the *way* we love. Probably one of the more subtle things that we inadvertently do as parents is use guilt and shame to control our children. Unfortunately the effects of using guilt and shame can live for a lifetime in our children's souls. Really. For those of us who were parented with even a small dose of guilt and shame, we bear the scars of that.

Of course none of us will be perfect parents, and there will be days when we fail in this area, yet this is the very thing God uses to help us remember our need for redemption and freedom through Christ. And these, by the way, are also things we want to pass on to our children!

In the Image of God

What if we were to begin to think and act differently today? How would we treat our children with love and respect in a way that would honor the image of God that has been imprinted on them? Think about it for a minute: How would you treat the presence of Christ in your midst? Of course, He is God and would be revered as holy, but to begin to think about that image of God in everyone He has created is a sobering thought.

This thought process compels me to assess every area of how I treat my children. How will I discipline them and still show love and respect? How will I celebrate them and listen to them and show love and respect? Love and respect are gifts we can give our children. They build trust, confidence, safety, and security. Our children will need all of these things to live productive and spiritually healthy lives.

What's Love Got to Do with It?

Sometimes I wonder if I really know what it means to love someone. I think I do. I say I do. But the standard for loving another is radically high. After all, Jesus said, "Greater love has no one than this, that he lay down his life for his friends" (John 15:13). Certainly we would say we love our children. We know they are gifts from God. Most of us would offer our lives for our children, without hesitation, if the moment called for it.

We financially, physically, and emotionally sacrifice for them every day. We hope for their best, and we endure many toddler and teen years when others want nothing to do with these offspring of ours. But in the end is this *enough* for them to know they are loved? Will they be shaped in an environment of love that will ultimately give them the ability to love God and others?

From 1 Corinthians 13 we know that love is patient, kind, self-sacrificing, neither self-seeking nor envious. It endures, hopes, and trusts. Stop for a moment and ask yourself, "Which of these aspects of love am I already doing consistently in my relationship with my children? Which are hard for me?" To love like this is to love the way God loves me. I want to love my children *that way*. Of course, I know I fall short, and that drives me to a deeper gratitude for God's grace and a deeper dependence on the Holy Spirit. I need His help so that I can grow in loving my children in this amazing way.

Jesus said this is the greatest of all the commandments: "'Love the Lord your God with all your heart and with all your soul and with all your mind and with all your strength.' The second is this: 'Love your neighbor as yourself.' There is no commandment greater than these" (Mark 12:30–31).

John tells us, "We love because he first loved us" (1 John 4:19). So in order for our children to be successful lovers of God and others, they must experience what love is for themselves. True love. Genuine love. The kind of love designed by God Himself.

The God Kind of Love

I make a mistake when I think, "Of course I love my children," and I don't count the cost of what that requires of me. In order to do this, it will be necessary for me to ask God every day to help me love my children the way He would love them if He were here physically parenting them. Wow!

I remember the first moments of holding my daughter and my son. There was this instant bond of love that covered us. In that moment, I knew I would do anything for those little babies. Each of them was so helpless and pure. Never would it have dawned on me to pray for God to *help me* love them. I simply thought I did. I didn't start seriously praying until they grew and I realized the enormous responsibility that was mine—either to shape their heart with love or to shape it with love's counterfeit, something that might look like love but failed to offer the full extent of what God intended.

We may be tempted to think sacrificial love is running at a hectic pace to get our children to every sporting event under the sun, spending outrageous amounts of money on new clothes and trendy toys, or overcontrolling every detail of their lives so they won't make a mistake. Other homes have even more dysfunctional forms of counterfeit love, such as verbal abuse, manipulation, guilt, and treating children as peers. These are all counterfeits, because they are dictated by our agenda instead of God's value system.

Many of us were raised by parents who offered authentic love. The Greek word for this is *agape*—a love that is unconditional, self-sacrificing, and active. This kind of love is divine. Others of us were raised in homes where we were told we were loved but were neglected instead. As children this would have been very confusing for us—to hear one thing but experience another.

Still others of us, out of our love for our parents (who might not have been capable of *agape* love at the time) had to become the caregivers. Finally, some of us may have been raised in homes where words of love were rarely, if ever, uttered. We may have known it was there (or not), but it would have made all the difference to have heard those words spoken.

Childhood wounds of love run deep. So deep that we inadvertently pass them on from generation to generation unless we are diligent to unpack the heritage we have been given, take assessment, and allow God to create a different future through us.

Take a moment to reflect about the love in your home of origin. Whether you had a home full of love or whether you did not, you can experience God's love and learn from it. You can receive the love that God wants you to offer to your children.

A Man Named Ron Van Groningen

I know a man named Ron Van Groningen. His story may not be much different from your own or that of someone you know, but it has taught me how love is transferred from generation to generation.

When Ron was a little boy in the early 1940s, his father went off to war, as many fathers did at that time. His mom was left to struggle during the Depression to care for him and his little brother on the meager means of what she alone could earn. Because she had ongoing health issues, Ron's mother was often just doing her best to get by.

When Ron's dad returned from the war, the world felt like a very different place to him. He had a difficult time readjusting to home life as a husband and father without some of the resources we have available for soldiers today. This young family desperately needed his love and attention, but they did not receive it. Not once did Ron ever hear the words "I love you, Son" from the lips of his father.

Soon the pressures of trying to reenter a forgotten world became too much, and Ron's father sought another woman's comfort and left his family behind. The stigma of being a divorcée during the early 1950s was cruel for Ron's mother, and the impact of being fatherless cut deeply into the two brothers' hearts over the years.

Without a Father's Love?

Ron's mother had to take on more odd jobs and find work as a woman who had never graduated from high school. As other young boys rode off in buses to baseball camp, Ron sat on his porch watching them pass by, unable to attend because he didn't have the money to buy even a baseball mitt.

When adolescence arrived, there was no father around to show Ron how to navigate issues of image, dating, hormones, and work. Still, what hurt the most was that Ron couldn't understand how a father could not love his own son.

When Ron turned eighteen, graduated from high school, and joined the air force, he was left to figure out how to enter the world of manhood without the love and support of a father. He married young, put himself through medical school, worked two jobs, and supported his family of two little girls and a young wife all by himself.

Now statistics would say that Ron would have had trouble loving his wife and children and would have even left them for someone else eventually. But something was different in Ron's life that didn't allow statistics to be the final chapter. Ron had known love after all.

When Ron was just a boy, he had learned of God's love for him, and he had chosen to give his life to Christ. God brought circumstances, a wife, a job, schooling, provision, and love to this young man—shaping him every step of the way, most of the time without Ron's awareness. Ron had truly experienced *agape* from God.

Redeemed by Love

While he was raising his two daughters, not a day went by when they were not showered with words of affirmation and love. The phrase "I love you" was used generously and without reserve. He demonstrated love to his wife and modeled what it meant to be a husband and father in every way.

When there were tears, he was there to hold the one crying and give encouraging words and tender hugs. When there were scary nights of lightning and thunder, he told stories until peaceful sleep returned. When there were mistakes made, he gave grace and forgiveness generously.

Ron has been married for forty-eight years. His grown daughters, his wife, and his grandchildren characterize him as a man who loves. Was it modeled to him by his father in his family of origin? No. Did he wish it had been? Yes. Yet God did the impossible and made a father from the fatherless. He does it every day. He redeems that which was lost.

I love the story of Ron Van Groningen, because it is a story of redemption and God's amazing intervening love. But mostly I love this story because that man is my father. I was the recipient of that unbelievable gift of love and know firsthand that God can use whatever past we bring to Him in order to offer love to our children and our children's children.

Love and Acceptance

As we offer God's kind of love to our children, we must be diligent to love the way He loves. We have the responsibility to train them how to live by using *this kind* of love. Training can be difficult, because the very nature of course correction makes one feel a sense of negativity.

I hate to discipline my children. I feel frustrated—they feel frustrated. I feel angry—they feel angry. I feel exasperated—they feel exasperated. Little about the process *feels* great. In the midst of training our children, it is dangerous to confuse two things that ought never to be misunderstood. We shouldn't confuse *loving a person* with *accepting a behavior*. We can communicate that we reject a behavior without communicating that we reject the person. When behavior is unacceptable, our words need to be clear that we reject the choice and the action, but we love the person.

My children will misbehave, they will sin, they will make bad choices. Fact! We all know this about our children, yet why are we so surprised when they do? It's easy for me to simply withhold love when they fail, because I don't find their behavior acceptable. I may not verbally say I am withholding love, but my actions can say it powerfully.

Getting What You Deserve

One day after my preteen daughter and I had experienced a bitter battle of the wills, she ran up to her room screaming that she wished she lived somewhere else. At that point I may have agreed with her—just for a moment. But I realized that my daughter needed my love in that very moment more than she needed to go to her room and think about what she had done and said.

My flesh wanted her to stay in her room until she felt sorry enough for what she had done and was ready to come to me to apologize. I wanted her to feel the separation of our relationship and to just "sit in it" for a while. After all, she deserved to feel bad, right?

Then, a tender voice inside reminded me of the words from Romans 5:8: "But God demonstrates his own love for us in this: While we were *still sinners*, Christ died for us." It was like a ton of bricks had just hit me! "While we were still sinners" played over and over in my mind as I wrestled with God about what to do.

Slowly, I opened my daughter's door and walked in. She was sitting on her bed in tears. She barked at me, "What are *you* doing here?" I recoiled, thinking that she didn't deserve my love in that moment. But God kept prompting me.

I said, "I'm here because I love you and I want to be with you, even though you have made a poor decision and you're angry at me." She was surprised. "How can you want to be with me right now, when I don't even want to be with me?" she asked through her tears.

I sat with her and held her. I told her that although her actions were not acceptable, she was dearly loved and I would always want her in my life—no matter what!

Love and Repentance

She did apologize and asked for my forgiveness. I remembered Romans 2:4: "Or do you show contempt for the riches of his kindness, tolerance and patience, not realizing that *God's kindness leads you toward repentance?*" There are times when we must go to our children purely because they don't deserve it. We must show kindness and love when they are certain they will receive our wrath. We must give grace because this reflects the absolute paradox of loving the way God loves instead of loving the way the world loves.

I believe love like this shapes the heart of a child toward being able to begin to comprehend the incomprehensible love of the heavenly Father. When they're older, and their sins have much greater consequences and depth of pain, will they hide in some secret place all alone in guilt and shame, or will they say, "I know—I will go to my Father, because He will accept me and love me," and run straight to His arms (see Luke 15:17–20)? I want my children to run to Him, not away from Him. What about you?

Listen with Generosity

Not only does love shape our children in profound and personal ways, but it is also informed by how we show it. Respect offers a context for this love—respect for our children. Now at first this may seem odd. We all know that children should respect their parents, but the concept of parents respecting their children is more foreign. But as we saw earlier, this respect for our children comes from the profound understanding that our children were made in the image of God. One practical way to show respect to our children is to listen to them.

There's listening and there's *listening,* right? But even greater, there is listening *generously.* Whether it is with your spouse or your children, listening with generosity is a gift we give them. This is the kind of listening that tracks with them and asks clarifying questions, such as, "What did you mean by that?" or, "Are you saying this?" or, "What I heard you say is … and let me clarify this."

We show respect when we look into our children's eyes when they are talking to us. I think of how often I said, "Look at me when I'm talking to you," but didn't look at my children with that same intent when they were talking to me. Did I look at my son and listen generously when he wanted to show me the Curious George book for the umpteenth time? Did I look at my daughter when she was telling me about her day at school? Did I listen to them? Did I listen generously?

A Lesson in Fatherhood

One of the most beautiful examples of parenting our children with this kind of respect comes from a moment I had the privilege of observing when my friend Mike was with his son one day.

Along with many other families, Mike and his family had gone up to the mountains to help clean the local camp in order to get it ready for the hundreds of children who would be participating in summer camp that season. The camp had seen one of the rainiest seasons ever recorded, which had left pinecones and needles littering the camp from edge to edge. This abundance of debris made a great potential for fires. It was our job, therefore, to rake, gather, and bag the forest debris into large piles where the tractor could scoop them up and pile them for removal.

Mike was driving the tractor most of the day. He claims he was being a servant, but we all knew he was feeling pretty powerful in that mammoth of a machine. He took great care in shoveling the huge piles of needles and cones with what seemed one effortless maneuver of the controls.

Now Mike has a son with a developmental disorder who was five years old at the time. His son loved watching his dad on the tractor—from afar. At one point Mike stopped working, left the tractor, and took a short break. When he returned, his son was standing just a few feet from the tractor. We had all stopped working to wait for the tractor to take away the debris that had piled up. "Daddy, drive the tractor," his son yelled. "Drive it, Daddy!" Mike was excited to see his son's enthusiasm. So he jumped up on the seat and started the powerful engine.

Seeing Eye to Eye

Mike's son was instantly terrified by the loud sound that came from the tractor, and Mike saw his son begin to scream. It would have been so easy for him to just drive off, realizing how many people were waiting for him, or to point to his wife and shuffle his son off to his mom. He could have yelled out to any of us to comfort his son or take care of the situation.

But instead, while everyone was waiting, he turned off the engine. He got off and came down to his crying son. This six-foot-two, massive man got down on his knees to his son's level. He made eye contact and said, "Hey, buddy, did that sound scare you?" His son said with a whimper, "Yeah." Then Mike said, "Oh, I'm so sorry about that." He went on, "I have an idea, why don't you go with your mom, and I'm going to start up the tractor again—so it's going to be loud, but if you want to put your hands over your ears, that's great. Or you can walk a little bit farther away so it won't be as loud. And then I'm going to drive the tractor, and it's going to be really cool. I'm going to pick up all the cones and needles, and then I'll see you in a little bit, okay?"

With that, he got back on the tractor, his son covered his ears, and Mike started up the engine and drove away while his smiling son watched him until he could no longer see the tractor.

Lasting Impact

I stood in amazement watching this tender story take place. It may seem like a simple example to you, but when I think of how often we all take the other options available to us—and how easily we justify them—we probably can't begin to understand the profoundness of love and respect that took place in this sweet interchange.

It's true that we were all waiting, but we were waiting for only sixty seconds! Believe me, we were *all* willing to wait sixty seconds for this man to show respect to his son. We may never know what impact that moment will have or could have had if he had handled it otherwise. This was not a huge life-and-death moment—he could have justified handling this differently, and none of us would have judged him for it. We would never have given it a second thought—and yet maybe his son *would* have.

In the Bedrock

I love to watch parents who are willing to get down at their child's level and make sure they have eye contact and a loving touch.

They make sure they're having a conversation *with* another human being—and it's so powerful. And the benefit comes in your children knowing you love and respect them.

Then when puberty and the teenage years begin, you've cultivated a bedrock of love and respect that is foundational to their adult relationship with you. Remember the law of sowing and reaping? If you sow love and respect into your child, you will reap the harvest of a teenager who wants to show you love and respect. This is not a science, of course. This is not "if you do this, then they will automatically do this" mathematics. But in the families I have observed whose parents showed their children love and respect, I witness the older children giving it back to the parents.

John Westerhoff cautions us, "Of course, it is easier to impose than reflect, easier to instruct than share, easier to act than to interact. It is important, however, to remember that to be with a child in Christian ways means self-control more than child-control. To be Christian is to ask: What can I bring to another? Not: What do I want that person to know or be? It means being willing to learn from another, even a child."[18]

Show It First

We should show it *first* and expect it *next*. So many parents complain to me about their disrespectful teenagers, trying to demand and command respect from the very children to whom they didn't give respect in the early years.

Now if you have older children, and you failed in love and respect in the early years, you can begin today by sitting down and having this conversation with your older child or teenager:

You know, I've been thinking about the way our relationship has been going for the last few years. I haven't always treated you with respect, and I want to change that. God has placed this on my heart, and I want to treat you with the respect you deserve because you were created by God and for His pleasure.

Will you tell me the kinds of things that I do or say to you that make you feel disrespected? Because I want to change those. I want to improve in those areas. And if you can't think of them right now, and I do something in the future that makes you feel disrespected, will you respectfully tell me that?

Now, you're not in charge and I am still the parent, so there might be things that you feel are disrespectful but they're not, so we'll have to have a conversation about those in order to determine which are which. Is that fair? I love you, and I want to love and respect you the way God does so that I accurately reflect His love to you.

You can start creating a new environment. You can set out on a new path and show your children the respect they need. Show it first and expect it next.

This environment of love and respect demands more of me than I have available in my own strength. Therefore, it compels me to rely on God's Spirit. Only He can make me love my children in a way that affirms His image in them. Only God can help me to pass on His kind of love, to show respect in the way I discipline, speak, and listen to their lives. As I let Him do these things through me, I also have the opportunity to understand in greater ways the love God has for me and the grace He extends to me simply because I am His. This deep understanding, far deeper than simply having knowledge *about* God, is something both my children and I need to experience in the environment of knowing.

11

A True Relationship
The Environment of Knowing

We know God as we build a relationship with
Him. He has beckoned us to come, and we have
accepted His invitation. Along the way we interact,
dialogue, and commune. Some days are filled with
excitement and discovery while others are quiet
and contemplative. Our relationship is anything
but predictive, but as we "do life together" we
feel alive and encouraged by His presence.

Michael Anthony

To Know and Be Known

When I was growing up, my mom had this special ability to make me
feel known. Not just me, but anyone who was fortunate enough to
be in relationship with her. She listened to me with endless devotion,

making sure she knew exactly what I was saying. She was aware of the smallest nuances of what was happening in my life, and she let me know she cared. Now as an adult, I see that she gives this gift of attentiveness to all who are in her life. She pays careful attention to every gift, card, and word that she offers, and her recipients feel known.

Deep inside us we all want to be known, and beyond that, loved for who we are. God's Word proclaims that no one knows us better than God—and no one loves us more either! Psalm 139 describes how He knows us from our conception:

> O LORD, you have searched me
>   and you know me.
> You know when I sit and when I rise;
>   you perceive my thoughts from afar.
> You discern my going out and my lying down;
>   you are familiar with all my ways.
> Before a word is on my tongue
>   you know it completely, O LORD.
> You hem me in—behind and before;
>   you have laid your hand upon me.
> Such knowledge is too wonderful for me,
>   too lofty for me to attain....
> For you created my inmost being;
>   you knit me together in my mother's womb.
> I praise you because I am fearfully and wonder-
>   fully made;
>   your works are wonderful,
>   I know that full well.

> My frame was not hidden from you
>> when I was made in the secret place.
> When I was woven together in the depths of the
> earth,
>> your eyes saw my unformed body.
> All the days ordained for me
>> were written in your book
>> before one of them came to be. (vv. 1–6, 13–16)

In addition, Jesus shouts out God's great love for us:

> "For God so loved the world that he gave his one
> and only Son, that whoever believes in him shall
> not perish but have eternal life. For God did not
> send his Son into the world to condemn the world,
> but to save the world through him." (John 3:16–17)

Greatest Defining Moment

Jesus never ceased to tell stories of how great the Father's love is for each of us. But God didn't leave it at that. He didn't leave it at an almighty God knowing and loving His creation; He also *chose to make Himself known to us*. What an incredible thought! The God of this universe says we can *know* Him. This is the greatest defining moment of our entire lives: when we come to know God personally. This is the moment when everything changes.

Certainly there are things about an infinite God that our finite minds can't comprehend—this is what makes Him God. Yet the

Bible tells us over and over again that we can know who He is, comprehend what He is like, and understand His character. He has chosen to reveal Himself in small and grand ways.

Take a look at these statements from the Bible:

- "*Know* therefore that the LORD your God is God; he is the faithful God, keeping his covenant of love to a thousand generations of those who love him and keep his commands" (Deut. 7:9).
- 'You are my witnesses,' declares the LORD, 'and my servant whom I have chosen, so that you may *know* and believe me and understand that I am he. Before me no god was formed, nor will there be one after me' (Isa. 43:10).
- "I keep asking that the God of our Lord Jesus Christ, the glorious Father, may give you the Spirit of wisdom and revelation, so that you may *know* him better" (Eph. 1:17).

Each of these passages affirms not only that God desires to make Himself known to us, but that there is no other true God besides Him to know.

Is God Real?

I remember the time my daughter came running into the house, telling me that our neighbor had just told her he didn't believe in God. She was crying, and through her sobs she whimpered that this neighbor had asked her that if God was real, why couldn't she ever see Him or hear Him speak? He mocked her, "Have you ever seen Him? Have you ever heard His voice?"

I was saddened that this doubt had been put in my daughter's mind. But even more than that, for a moment I felt the responsibility of *proving* that God existed and that she *could* see Him and hear Him. But God gently reminded me that this was something He would be faithful to do and that it was my job merely to put my daughter in the environment where she would best be able to experience Him.

Contrast to the World

The environment of knowing stands in sharp contrast to what the world says is true. The world says there is no God, and if there is, He is irrelevant. The world says there is no Creator and no absolute truth. As followers of Christ, we are saying, "Yes, there is, and you can know Him—you can know God the Father through His Son Jesus in the power of His Spirit." There is absolute truth, and His Word is truth. It trumps all experiences and all counterfeits.

In this environment we stand firm and are confident in our relationship with God through Jesus and confident of His Word as the reliable source of truth for transforming lives. Throughout the history recorded in the Bible, God confirmed this reliability by orchestrating events in order that people would *know* that He alone was God. The phrase "so that you might know that I [alone] am God" is recorded over a hundred times in His Word.

In the environment of knowing, the Holy Spirit can work because our kids are watching us. They're watching to see if we say one thing about God's Word and then do another, or if we say we should trust God in all things but as soon as that is put to the test, we panic. Do we go to the world's resources, or do we drop to our knees and pray? Do we go to God's Word for instruction or pick up another self-help book? When you know someone and you trust them, you will go to them. We can train our children how to do this through knowing who God is personally, as revealed in His Word and through His Spirit.

Natural Discovery

Moses addresses this concept in Deuteronomy 6, in what is known in Hebrew as the *Shema*. This is the first prayer a child learns in a Jewish home and the words they hear every night at bedtime. God reveals through Moses that faith teaching occurs best in the *natural daily flow of life*—from the living examples of parents who are modeling it. In the *Shema*, Moses says,

> Hear, O Israel: The LORD our God, the LORD is
> one. Love the LORD your God with all your heart
> and with all your soul and with all your strength.
> These commandments that I give you today are
> to be upon your hearts. Impress them on your
> children. Talk about them when you sit at home
> and when you walk along the road, when you lie
> down and when you get up. Tie them as symbols
> on your hands and bind them on your foreheads.
> Write them on the doorframes of your houses and
> on your gates. (Deut. 6:4–9)

Moses commissions the parents *first* to be lovers of God with everything that is within them, and *then* to pass this very compelling faith down to their children in the everyday occurrences of life. This is the natural flow of our lives. How ridiculous would it be if every morning I said to my children, "Come let me tell you about God," and we had a formal Sunday school moment or something like it, but that was the only time I ever talked to them about God?

Rather, the *Shema* says learning to know God happens best in the natural flow of life. This means that teaching our children who God is does not happen only in the environment of storytelling, when we sit them down and say, "Now I will tell you the great mysteries of God." We need to do that, but the natural flow of their lives offers the most fertile soil for knowing God personally. Every single opportunity, every single hour that we are given in a day, is an opportunity for our children to discover who God is.

Through My Parents' Eyes

When I was a child, my parents did a great job of pointing my eyes toward God. They intentionally created environments for me to get to know God in meaningful ways. My mother has a love for the splendor in creation. She reacted to things in nature as if it were the first time she was seeing them. Her awe of God's handiwork made my eyes more attentive to the God who is the artist behind the canvas of life. To this day, whenever the sun is setting I have to run out and watch it because of the way my mother cued me to view it as God's painting the sky a different way every single day!

My dad was especially interested in insects, rocks, and vegetation. He said, "Look at the intricacies of this insect. Isn't it amazing how God did that?" Or he brought my attention to how God made the giraffe, the zebra, and the leopard with their spots and stripes so they could hide from aggressors in the jungles and plains. He told me how the ocean was salty so it wouldn't completely freeze and how it used the salt to purify itself. In all of these ways, my parents revealed God as Creator to me—a Creator who is intimately involved in His creation ... and I am His beloved creation too.

Knowing God's Voice

In John 10, Jesus says, "I am the good shepherd; I know my sheep and my sheep know me—just as the Father knows me and I know the Father—and I lay down my life for the sheep" (vv. 14–15). Remember the goals of spiritual parenting we set in chapter 1—to put our children in the path of the Divine so that they would learn to:

- *hear* and *know* God's voice,
- *desire* to obey it,
- *obey* it in the power of God's Spirit (not their own strength).

These are powerful things! There are so many young people in our churches, in our neighborhoods and communities, who can't say any of these things are true for them. Since they can't hear and know God's voice, the by-product of knowing—obedience from a pure heart—is impossible. We don't obey because of knowledge; we obey out of relationship!

This very fact is the reason why our children are tempted to "perform" obedience to please us rather than have an authentic relationship with God that empowers them to align their behavior to His will. And other children, when they don't discern God's voice, conclude that He isn't real and decide to abandon faith living altogether.

Because they don't understand God's voice directing them in a spiritual sense, they often can't discern between the shouting voice of the world and what God might be telling them. Add to this the fact that young people aren't known for having wills eager to obey, and following God is even more difficult. As our children get older, only God and the transformation He brings will give them a heart of obedience.

The bottom line is that both we and our children need to learn to understand God's voice through knowing who He is. As we learn to know His character and those things that bring Him sadness or pleasure, we learn how to live our lives accordingly. His Word and His Spirit act as guides for us to understand what it means to live in relationship with God our Father.

Messengers of Good News

These are critically profound things, and as we've discussed, they start with knowing. The apostle Paul said, "How beautiful are the feet of those who bring good news!" (Rom. 10:15). We are meant to be messengers of good news to our children. God has sent us into our families, to our specific children, to share it—and then when they hear it, the goal is for them to *know* God personally. Paul's whole context in 10:14–15 is the environment of knowing, and while the church can aid us in this task, the church doesn't have enough time with our children to do the whole job.

My husband and I had the privilege of being the ones who brought this good news to our children and prayed with them to receive Christ. Those are moments I will never forget—our children's tender prayers asking Jesus to forgive their sin and inviting Him to begin a relationship with them. There is no greater joy than to give the good news to another, especially our children whom we love so dearly.

Spiritual Wisdom and Mighty Power

Paul prays this for the church in Ephesus:

> I keep asking that the God of our Lord Jesus Christ,
> the glorious Father, may give you the Spirit of
> wisdom and revelation, so that you may know him
> better. I pray also that the eyes of your heart may be
> enlightened in order that you may know the hope
> to which he has called you, the riches of his glorious
> inheritance in the saints. (Eph. 1:17–18)

He goes on to say in verses 19–22 that he wants us to understand the power that is ours in Christ and how this "power is like the working of his mighty strength, which he exerted in Christ when he raised him from the dead" (vv. 19–20)! That's an amazing amount of power! He then "seated him at his right hand in the heavenly realms, far above all rule and authority, power and dominion, and every title that can be given, not only in the present age but also in the one to come. And God placed all things under his feet and appointed him to be head over everything" (vv. 20–22).

I don't know about you, but these verses amaze me. And they also remind me that this power available to us is preceded by *knowing* God (Eph. 1:17). The same power that raised Christ from the dead! That's an enormous amount of power at our disposal through Christ.

Do my kids know this? Have I lived this truth in a way that allows them to know the reality of God instead of the cheap imitation that I so often portray?

Our Hope and Calling

Knowing God includes knowing the hope to which He's called us. What a great prayer to have for our children! I long for my children to know Him and therefore to know the hope of their calling—this is the essence of why each of us is here on earth.

This knowledge answers epic questions: "Who is God? How has He anointed me to live my life? What's my calling? What's my purpose here on earth?" The hope of our calling, through the power of Christ, is the reason we live and breathe. We each have a special part to play in God's grand narrative. As my children have grown older, I can see that these are the fundamental questions they wrestle with. It's imperative that I equip them to know where to go for the answers to those questions!

Knowing God versus Knowing About God

We are raising our children in a world that denies absolute truth. Yet God's Word offers just that. As we create an environment that upholds and displays God's truth, we give children a foundation that is based on knowing God, believing His Word, and having a relationship with Him through Christ. These are essentials for our faith, and they all begin with knowing God.

It's easy to get swept away with the tide of knowing *about* God. We can memorize a host of Bible verses and facts and still not truly know God. This was true of the religious people of Jesus' day, and it can be true today if we're not cautious. Knowing God must always be the center of all we do.

When I was in sixth grade, my Sunday school teacher challenged our class to memorize as many verses as we could over a period of four months. The person who memorized the most verses would win a brand-new Bible. This Bible was called *The Way*, and it was a paraphrase of the Bible that I really wanted, so I started memorizing. Each week I rattled off my verses to my teacher, and he marked how many I had recited. When the four months came to a close, I was the victor!

The day came for me to receive my reward, and I was called to the front of the chapel to receive my new Bible. My teacher asked me one poignant question: "Michelle, we are so proud of you for all of your hard work, but my question to you is this—how are you different because of hiding God's Word of truth in your heart?" I just stood there in shock. *Different? Wait, that wasn't the challenge! You didn't say anything about change—I just thought I was supposed to memorize the verses.*

Looking back, I'm grateful that I memorized those verses. To this day, the bulk of God's Word that I have hidden in my heart can be traced back to that summer in sixth grade. I'm also grateful for a teacher who perceived my pride in accomplishing a great task but desired more for me. He desired that I would know the very God whose words I had memorized.

Truth Is Essential to Knowing God

In our world, people think truth is relative to perception, opinion, and experience. In Romans 1:25, Paul speaks about the depravity we have in our society as a result of *exchanging the truth of God for a lie*.

Paul just calls it out. He says the reason we live in so much disarray and debauchery is that the truth of God is evident before us, but we deny it and exchange it for a lie! And after working with young people for the last twenty years, that is exactly what I've witnessed. Young people will exchange the truth of God for a lie—and so will we if we're not vigilant!

When our children have a vacuum of truth in their lives, they will accept a lie, because that feels more real to them than anything else. As spiritual parents, we choose to inspire them by constantly reminding them that there is capital-T Truth. And we make it compelling by living it out before them in honest and authentic ways, in real time. We must share the truth we are experiencing today, not just recount truth that we learned or experienced ten or fifteen years ago.

Jesus says He alone is the truth, and no man comes to the Father except through Him (John 14:6). Furthermore, the truth He offers will set us free (John 8:32)! Our children are inspired when they begin to see the correlation between the capital-T Truth and freedom. Unfortunately the church has often packaged capital-T Truth as a path that leads to bondage. Somehow we have communicated that we are unable to do positive things, that we are trapped, and that therefore we define ourselves by those things that we *don't* do. That rigid list of don'ts is bondage.

But when our children see that truth actually leads to freedom, they begin to taste what Jesus meant when He said, "I have come that they may have life, and have it to the full" (John 10:10). What young person doesn't want the full life with true freedom? These are words they will run *to* instead of *away from*, if they know the God who said them and if they see us live by them.

The Importance of Knowing

Still, there's an aspect of the environment of knowing that is sobering. In Romans 1, Paul argues that while the things we see in God's
creation are enough to condemn us, they're not enough to save us.
We live in a world where God's attributes are clearly seen, so we are
without excuse.

Thus, we need to create an environment that shows our children
not only how to know God but also what *saves them* from condem-
nation. What saves is the incarnate Christ. The Holy Spirit comes
into their lives to redeem what was sinful and lost to bring fullness
and freedom. It has been vital for me as a parent to make sure I am
putting my child in proximity to God in order that he will know the
God of truth, and that through Him, he will be free to fulfill God's
plan for his life.

This environment of knowing, and all of the environments, are
linked to one final environment: modeling. We've seen that faith
teaching occurs best in the daily flow of life—from the living examples of parents who are modeling it.

12

What I Say Is What I Do
The Environment of Modeling

The best things your children will learn about
God will be from watching you try to find out
for yourself. Jesus said, "Seek and you will find."
They will not always do what you tell them to
do, but they will be—good and bad—as they
see you being. If your children see you seeking,
they will seek—the finding part is up to God.

Polly Berrien Berends[19]

Do as I Do

One of my favorite things about children is how they mimic almost
anything or anyone with great precision. When my kids were little, I
marveled at how they could imitate anyone from pop singers to car-
toon characters. It was especially funny when one imitated a family

member, candidly exposing their bad behavior, saying what we all wanted to say but couldn't.

However, it wasn't as funny when that child did something unpleasant that I had modeled by my actions. Once, upon correction, my daughter reminded me she was only doing what she had just witnessed me doing. She was right. I had been caught. I realized very quickly that raising children was like holding up a very large and animated mirror—and sometimes I didn't like what I saw!

There are times when we don't even realize the things we are passing down to our children just because they live among us and learn from us in every one of life's situations. Some of these things are commendable. For instance, my husband and I have passed down to my children an ability to interact with people of diverse ages, races, and cultures. We have traveled with our children in order to expose them to a variety of situations, modeling for them how to respond in a multitude of circumstances.

I also modeled how to keep a clean room by making my bed every morning and picking up the house before going to bed. These short accounts allowed our home to rarely have more clutter than what could be made in a day. My own mother had modeled this habit to *me,* making our home feel inviting and safe because it was orderly and clean.

Yet other things I've modeled are not so praiseworthy. I seem to consistently run about five to ten minutes late. I don't like this about myself, and today I try to be prompt. But as a young mom I modeled being late and not making time a priority. As a result, my daughter has struggled with this same issue, and it pains me to see her dealing with something that has been hard for me. My husband has a tendency to deal impatiently with the imperfect drivers on the highway, and my son, who has recently acquired his own license to drive, seems to share this same frustration.

Begin with the End in Mind

Perhaps this characteristic in children is why Paul said, "Be imitators of God, therefore, as dearly loved *children*" (Eph. 5:1). He knew the nature of children to imitate and desired that to be our posture before our heavenly Father. Imitating God is always a good thing. He is perfect. I can't fail when I choose to behave the way Christ modeled for us.

Yet as a parent, I am a frail and tainted example of that. My children will mimic me. And whether I like it or not, I am the primary role model in their life during the most formative years. Understanding the role I play is critical to me as I model not only life here in this world, but also what it means to live for a world to come. I have to ask myself, "What kinds of things do I want my kids to imitate? And how will I model those things in an intentional environment?" I must begin with the end in mind.

I think about how I am as a mother, wife, and friend today. I increasingly recognize how often I respond in the ways that my mother did. Sometimes it's intentional, and at other times I am completely unaware why or how I am doing something until later reflection. And then I realize I saw my mother model such integrity, joy, or tenacity, and that served as my inspiration.

We've discussed the concept of being a living role model for your children throughout this book. We've seen that we train our children to be servants by modeling servanthood to them. We've observed that if we model love and respect to our children when they are small, they will grow to be teens who love and respect us and others. There's a modeling component in nearly all of the environments. And if we model the opposite of servanthood or respect or one of the other environments, then our children tend to follow that model to their detriment.

The Whiteboard Story

I have often thought of my role in modeling like this:

> One day I took out a large whiteboard and wrote my child's name on it. Each day, I wrote down the kinds of things I hoped for her to attain. I wrote things such as: Love selflessly, give generously, follow Christ, love God, be patient in affliction, kindhearted and compassionate, prayerful, and pure in heart. Then I tried to model those things. Some days I was successful, and other days I utterly failed. Along the way I tried to show what was truth, even if I fell short.

> Then one day my daughter stood between me and the whiteboard. She held an eraser in her hand. I gasped as she walked over to the board and erased everything I had ever written. I knew it was time, and I had to let her choose for herself, but I was afraid.

> I watched as she wrote down her own words. Some of her words were the same as mine, but

others were different. I marveled at how much she remembered from what was erased. Then I realized that she had not only heard what I had said, but had been watching me over the years. This was her whiteboard now—she wrote the words, and I watched. It was her life now, but I had played a part in shaping it.

This story is bittersweet. We have been given a great privilege, and we have such a limited time to do it in. Spiritual parents recognize the brevity of our profound influence in our children's lives, and they choose to live their lives in that awareness.

Music and Lyrics

There is danger for the family that focuses its attention on pure content and creates an environment where it's hitting the knowledge part out of the ballpark but does not follow this up with congruent modeling. When I talk to young adults who were raised in Christian homes, I am always struck by the number of them who say, "Yeah, I don't really think the Christian thing works for me." And the more I pry into *why* they've said this, the more I hear it's because they have people in their life who say one thing and then do another.

Oftentimes these incongruent people are their parents, but sometimes they are the pastor or a youth leader. These students are looking to see if our words are congruent with our lifestyle. Singer-songwriter Ted Limpic once said, "Our lifestyle is the music that makes the lyrics of our song believable." I love that. A song is made up of music and lyrics—they need to fit.

Of course we're not perfect people. We're not perfect models—and we're not always going to be congruent. But what makes our ill behavior congruent in the environment of modeling is when we simply acknowledge that very fact. So we become a model whether we're modeling the correct way God would want us to do something or whether we're acknowledging that our behavior fell short. Honesty and humility in this area make us great models even when we fail. Now that's redemptive parenting!

A Living Example

When I was a little girl, my father had a problem with anger. As I described in chapter 10, he had been raised in a home where his dad left him, his brother, and his mom when he was only eight years old. In the early 1950s he was the only person in his community who didn't have a dad.

Added to this, his mother was often ill. He felt insecure and helpless. He and his little brother often went without, even though his mother worked several jobs to try to make ends meet. He heard her crying herself to sleep at night, and he cried too.

Over time this hurt must have built up inside of him as an enormous amount of bitterness and anger. Without the tools of psychology and the resources we have available today, my father entered early adulthood and even fatherhood with a substantial amount of baggage.

My dad, who was the most gentle, loving, and godly person I knew growing up, would also suddenly have enormous outbreaks of rage and anger. That was confusing for me as a little girl. He was a deacon in our church, and he was always pointing me to God.

Always displaying who God was. He was constantly praying and immersing himself in God's Word—but he also had these outbursts of anger.

One night we were having dinner together as a family when all of a sudden my father became very angry at my mom. He picked up his bowl of chili and threw it across the room. It crashed against the wall and shattered, sending pottery and chili everywhere. I was terrified. I ran up to my bedroom crying and shut my door.

It wasn't long before my father came and found me lying on my bed. I was maybe six years old, and he quietly entered and sat beside me. He knelt by my bed and just wept. He told me how sorry he was, and then he looked at me and said, "Michelle, I did not reflect God by my actions just then. Will you forgive me? That's not what Jesus would've done, and I'm sorry." I threw my arms around his neck and said, "Yes, Daddy, of course I forgive you."

Modeling in Our Mistakes

From a very early age I felt my dad was such a great example to me, even in his shortcomings and failures, because he consistently identified when his behavior was not congruent with that of Jesus. Moreover, he then modeled for me what to do when that happens: You go to the person, you ask for their forgiveness, and then you make it right.

This modeled for me that I didn't have to be perfect. It modeled that when I fall short, I need to take responsibility. This is a crucial part of parenting, because we are tempted to think of *modeling* in terms of a "standard." We think of it as some kind of perfection that we try to attain. Instead, we have the privilege of being a living, breathing model of grace when we fail and of grace when we get it right. Either way—we are compelled by grace! We model this truth as long as we make our words congruent with God's standards.

It isn't helpful when we fail and then try to cover it up. If my father had come to me that night and said, "Hey, I'm really sorry I threw the chili, but you know my dad left me when I was young, your mom's been nagging me all night, I was tired because I haven't slept, I was stuck in traffic—and so I'm just sorry that you were in the middle of that, but I've got a lot of stuff on my plate right now," how helpful would that have been? Yet how often do we do just that? How often do we make a litany of excuses for our bad behavior rather than just calling it what it is and seeking someone's forgiveness?

The Power of the Spirit

When I think about that incident with the chili bowl, I realize that it has, ironically, become one of my most treasured childhood memories. Why? Because beginning that day, my dad became a living, breathing example to me of the Holy Spirit's power—every day, every month, and every year since that moment, I've watched my dad rely on the Spirit to transform him. So much so that today he is the most gentle, loving, and patient man I know. This is not someone who has been merely "trying harder," but someone who has learned to abide in Christ and let the Holy Spirit transform him over time to be more like Jesus. My dad has been a living testament to me that God is real and that His power truly heals and transforms lives.

When I was a child, my mother didn't allow us to simply say, "I'm sorry," when one family member wronged another. She had us say, "I'm sorry—*will you forgive me?*" And then we'd have to wait for a response. It felt weird at the time, but looking back, I'm so glad that she enforced this. It was a good practice, because each time, I had to look at the family member whom I had offended in some way and know that my actions had wounded him or her. This was a practice in humility, and it cultivated in me accountability for my actions.

This simple practice also allows me to receive grace. Think about it: As I wait for the other person to respond (hopefully with a yes), I realize that I am in *relationship* with another person whom my actions affect. In essence, I'm saying, "As you offer forgiveness to me, please know that my intent is to not do that again, and I will try to rely on God's Spirit for that in the future."

Flesh on Faith

Modeling is the environment that creates a marriage with the other environments. It's a perfect union, since modeling demonstrates the "how" of the "what" that each environment reveals. In the other environments, we are challenged to learn about who God is and encouraged to live our lives in His power. Modeling gives us the opportunity to then show what that looks like by our actions to our watching children.

Think about the Old Testament for a minute. It describes so much about knowing God. It is full of His laws and nature. It reveals who God is! It's a declaration of His name and His identity. Then the New Testament comes along, and Jesus serves as the model for all the things we knew about God but were estranged from because of sin. Jesus came and modeled what it looked like to be in relationship with the Father. He was a living, breathing example.

Modeling answers the questions, "How do I practically put into practice what I have learned? How do I live in relationship with God and others? How do I obey God's Word? How do I abide in Christ? How do I let His Spirit guide me?" As parents, we become living, breathing examples of the answers to these questions. We put flesh on faith.

Relational Transformation

You might be thinking, "I'm not exactly sure how to do all these things myself, and therefore I don't feel confident modeling them for my children." This is not uncommon. Early in this book we discussed that it is nearly impossible to give away something we don't already possess. We recognized that the journey of the spiritual parent is first one of personal transformation. My hope is that each of us will never stop in this pursuit of knowing and following God—that we will never be tempted to believe we have "arrived." This humility will allow us to be leaders worthy of following for a lifetime.

The two concepts of *abiding in Christ* and *allowing His Spirit to guide our lives* are processes of spiritual growth. In any relationship, as we grow to know and understand the person we love, we grow in our understanding of how to best respond. The Christian life is all about responding to God. From the moment we choose to surrender our lives to God and accept the gift of salvation offered through Jesus, we begin the journey of relational transformation.

We learn about who God is through His Word, and we choose to follow Jesus' example by praying and asking God's Spirit to give us the strength to do what His Word says. Often as we discipline our lives and bodies through such things as spiritual disciplines (prayer, solitude, Scripture memory and meditation, fasting, community with others, confession, and so on), we begin to understand that self-denial and commitment to God's will for us create a path for hearing His voice in ways that we never could have imagined.

We seek God in prayer to reveal to us the blind spots and sin issues that hinder us from being good parents, and we acknowledge that without His help on a daily basis, surely we will fail. This type of dependence in prayer, on the Bible, and upon His Spirit (instead of our own fortitude) gives us the ability to model a life that has been surrendered to God for His glory—not our own.

A Lifetime of Influence

We have an ever-narrowing window of opportunity to maximize our influence in our children's lives. The fields of psychology and sociology tell us that we parents are the primary influencers in our children's lives from birth until twelve years old. Somehow this is almost a science. It's as if on the eve of their thirteenth birthday their brain chemistry changes in such a way that all of a sudden the world, music, media, and friends now become more influential than we are! I remember thinking this wouldn't happen to my sweet children— but it did! We must be shrewd to use this window of influence and capitalize on it in childhood. I don't want to give that influence to anybody else!

In fact, I want to extend my influence in my children's lives. We can say, "Well, sociology and psychology say I am the primary model for my kids from zero to twelve years, but by the grace of God I want to be an influence in my child's life until the day I die." I know this is possible because of my parents.

A Parent's Blessing

Several years ago I was going through a dark and difficult time in my life, both personally and professionally. I was sitting in a café talking to my husband when I began to cry. After sharing his comfort and thoughts with me, he said, "You know what you need? You need to go see your dad, listen to his wisdom, and have him bless you."

He picked up his cell phone, called a nearby airport, and got me on the next flight out. Just two hours later, I was on a plane flying up to San José to see my dad. I just showed up on his doorstep. He was totally surprised. I walked in. He said, "What is wrong? Is everything okay?" I began to cry, then said, "Yeah, I just needed to talk to you about some stuff."

Now here is this thirty-six-year-old woman, standing in her daddy's presence, wanting his blessing, wanting his wisdom. Somehow, by the way he had parented me, he had extended his influence past those first twelve years. What did he do? In what ways, even in his failures, did he model for me a life of pursuing Christ that made me want to seek him now? The key was his authenticity in which he lived. He was real.

We had dinner together. We talked. He prayed for me. I asked him for a blessing, and he gave it to me. Then he sent me on my way, and I was home before breakfast the next morning. I'm convinced we don't have to settle for only twelve years! We can parent in such a way that our children will come to us for wisdom and blessing for a lifetime.

Persevere to the End

As we endeavor to influence our children through our modeling, we must determine to persevere. Maybe this word sounds wearisome to you because you're persevering on so many fronts already. You may feel you are persevering through potty training, managing the car pool and homework schedules, or dealing with the teen years. But we must never forget that one of the most important things we do as spiritual parents is to persevere.

One of the sad realities of not persevering is the temptation to become a coaster parent. These are the parents who get their kids through about seventh or eighth grade, and then they simply *coast.* They're distracted with their career, their marriage (or the failure of their marriage), their economic situation—or they simply don't know what to do with high schoolers. They bail out, and by doing so they give up their influence to model. Each one of us, by God's grace, needs to persevere all the way through and fight to have a relationship, a *spiritual relationship,* with our children!

Empowered Responsibility

However, although I am responsible to God for my children, He has graciously offered me strength and wisdom to raise them (James 1:4–6). I am not alone. He in fact is the creator of my children. He knows them and loves them more than I do! What an incredible thought. He is the perfect parent who models for me how I should parent them.

So what is my response to the idea that I will stand before God one day to give an account? One possible response is fear. I may fear I'll do it wrong or get in trouble with God. Fear causes me to seek my own human strength and answers in order not to fail.

Another possible response is to recognize the enormity of my responsibility and then faithfully seek God for the wisdom and power I need but don't possess. In this response, I choose to rely on God to empower me to be the kind of parent Jesus would be, if He were me. I can do this by actively being in God's Word, in prayer, and in a community of others who want to spiritually parent their children as well. These build up a hedge around me as a parent.

Our souls grow spiritually when we have a chance to practice what God is revealing in a gracious environment where those who are spiritually mature can speak into our lives. These people, perhaps in our family or in our church, offer a safe place to pray together and to ask questions. Take a moment to think of those around you who can model this kind of parenting to you.

We Walk by Faith

This is the vision for us as spiritual parents: We persevere in loving Christ in our hearts and by our actions, in trusting in Him for what only He can give, and then modeling *this* to our children. We persevere, and we don't give up. We don't abdicate to somebody else. We don't make excuses for the way we were parented or the resources we didn't have. We walk by faith, and we thank God, the one who entrusted them to us in the first place. We fight the good fight *every day*, knowing that we can't model something that we don't already possess.

These are the very things we identified that we wanted for our children's faith development: (1) to *know and hear* God's voice through a loving relationship and through His Word, (2) to *desire* to obey His voice, and (3) to *obey* Him through the power of God's *Spirit* and not their own strength alone. You and your child are on a spiritual journey together, not just for the next few years, but for a lifetime, should God allow.

Take some time today to pray and ask God to empower you to parent in a way that strengthens your faith and that of your child. Perhaps you might want to pray a prayer like this:

Dear heavenly Father,

Thank You for entrusting these children to me. Thank You for giving me the privilege of pointing them to You, even though at times I feel so undeserving of this role. Help me to be a spiritual parent—with eyes to see what matters most to You.

I pray that You will show me how to create these environments in my home and in my life in ways that will reflect the truth of who You are to them. I want them to know You accurately and fully.

May our home be a place where truth and love prevail above all else, and may Your plans for my children, and myself, be fulfilled as we submit ourselves to Your desires. Please reveal Your desires to me, and craft my heart so that I will listen and obey. I trust Your Spirit to guide me and give me the wisdom and power to do the things that You desire.

I am Yours. Our home is Yours. These children are Yours. Be glorified!

Amen.

My Ahas from This Book

Notes

1. Donald Miller, *Blue Like Jazz* (Nashville: Thomas Nelson, 2003), 205.

2. George Barna, *Transforming Children into Spiritual Champions* (Ventura, CA: Regal, 2003), 12.

3. Helen Lemmel, "Turn Your Eyes upon Jesus," 1922.

4. Dallas Willard, *Divine Conspiracy,* (San Francisco: Harper Collins, 1997), 57.

5. Merton Strommen and Richard Hardel, *Passing on the Faith* (Winona, MN: Saint Mary's Press, 2000), 85.

6. John Westerhoff, *Will Our Children Have Faith?* (Harrisburg, PA: Morehouse Publishing, 2000), 32.

7. Ibid.

8. Ken Gire, *Windows of the Soul* (Grand Rapids, MI: Zondervan, 1996), 48.

9. Nancy Pearcey, *Total Truth* (Wheaton, IL: Crossway Books, 2004), 87, 89.

10. Max Lucado, *In the Grip of Grace* (Nashville: Thomas Nelson, 1996), 144.

11. Catherine Stonehouse, *Joining Children on the Spiritual Journey* (Grand Rapids, MI: Baker Academic, 1998), 37.

12. Strommen and Hardel, *Passing on the Faith,* 166.

13. Dallas Willard, *The Spirit of the Disciplines* (New York: HarperCollins, 1988), 182.

14. Francis Chan, *Crazy Love* (Colorado Springs, CO: David C. Cook, 2008), 122.

15. Miller, *Blue Like Jazz*, 107.

16. Henri Nouwen, *Finding My Way Home* (Cincinnati, OH: St. Anthony Messenger Press, 2007), 33.

17. Gire, *Windows of the Soul*, 36.

18. Westerhoff, *Will Our Children Have Faith?*, 17.

19. Polly Berrien Berends, *Gently Lead* (New York: HarperCollins, 1991), 9.

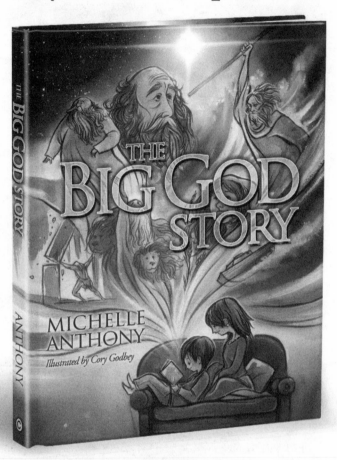